Praise for the Book

'Dr Abhishek Manu Singhvi is a lawyer with the Teflon touch. This book is for both non-lawyers and lawmen. The diversity of causes that he has represented through the journey of these cases makes compulsive reading. These cases represent milestones in the legal history of our country. A must-read.' **Kapil Sibal, member of Parliament and former Additional Solicitor General of India**

'The idea behind this book – of enlightening the lay reader about the vital role of the Supreme Court in almost every aspect of our contemporary life – is laudable. These diverse cases – argued by one of our foremost legal practitioners – are described in a simple and lucid style, encapsulating stories very well told.' **Soli Sorabjee, former Attorney General for India**

'The diversity of the legal themes covered in this legal journey for the non-lawyer is truly impressive and enlightening. Controversial contemporary social themes like Jallikattu and Sabarimala compete with imparted corporate issues like the Mistry–Tata dispute. The book also traverses hardcore constitutional adjudication having a heavy political flavour (e.g., Uttarakhand and Karnataka). Written by an eminent jurist and a third-term member of Parliament, this is a must-read for the expert, connoisseur and dilettante alike.' **K. Parasaran, former Attorney General for India**

'For many years now "Manu" Singhvi has been at the top of the profession of practising advocates, constantly arguing cases of someone or the other in India's highest court. In an account of eight such cases, he gives us what he has himself described as a "view from the trenches": well worth reading, not only because of a first-hand account of the foot soldier engaged in the conflict, but also because each of the eight pieces has been composed in elegant prose.' Fali S. Nariman, former president, Bar Association of India

From the Trenches

From the Trenches

Abhishek Singhvi

with
Satyajit Sarna

🌸 juggernaut

JUGGERNAUT BOOKS
KS House, 118 Shahpur Jat, New Delhi 110049, India

First published by Juggernaut Books 2020

10 9 8 7 6 5 4 3 2 1

P-ISBN: 9789353450908
E-ISBN: 9789353450915

Typeset in Adobe Caslon Pro by R. Ajith Kumar, Noida

Printed at Thomson Press India Ltd

To my mother
for her love and discipline
and
to my wife
for being an inseparable part of my life

Contents

Contents

Introduction

You are holding in your hand a collection of stories from my life as a counsel. Since 1981, I have argued for litigants in every kind of case – civil, criminal, commercial, constitutional, from the Supreme Court all the way down. I have argued before small tribunals in far-off corners of the country and I have argued in international arbitrations. I have won and I have lost. But above all I have learnt – and I am still learning. The law is a tough teacher.

Over these forty years, I have had the good fortune to have been involved in some of India's biggest legal battles. Not all of them lend themselves to a popular audience, but there are some that do catch the eye of the public. This is a selection of a few of those cases that might be interesting to the reader. Any such selection is necessarily short and arbitrary, for reasons of space, content and variety.

You may have read in the newspapers about cases I was involved in like Sabarimala, Jallikattu, or the fight between the Tata Group and Cyrus Mistry. Some of them you may not have heard of, but they laid down protections you benefit from, as, for example, freedom from custodial violence or expanded boundaries for freedom of speech.

Others are battles of public law, where the rights of a person or group of people are pitted against the government or the law. For example, do you as a private citizen have the right to fly the flag above your home? I have not in this book focused on too many commercial battles because while they are technically very interesting, they do not personally affect as many people.

Before we go any further, it may serve us well to discuss a few fundamental concepts here:

1. **The Constitution of India:** Our Constitution is the fundamental framework of rules that governs our entire political, civic and legal order as a nation. It lays down the basic principles for the functioning of the executive, the legislature and the judiciary. It lays down that India is a democracy, and how that democracy is to function,

with Houses of Parliament and elections. It lays down a structure which is federal in nature, that is, where there is a Central government and state governments, each of which can carry out different areas of governance. It states what our basic freedoms are and how they can be protected. Where a law or a governmental action falls afoul of the Constitution, that law or action is illegitimate and a court is to strike it down. Therefore, the Constitution functions as the supreme law of our country. But it is wrong to look at the Constitution as unchangeable, or cast in stone. Judicial interpretations, coupled with the changing mores of society, attach new and ever-changing meanings and facets to the principles in different articles. This is why we call it a living document.

2. **Writ petition:** A writ petition is an action by which a person seeks relief from the courts against actions of a government or a public authority. Under the Constitution, writ petitions can be filed in High Courts and in the Supreme Court. They are a kind of remedy originating in medieval times where the essential fairness of an authority's actions could be challenged before a judicial authority. The person who files a writ petition is a petitioner and the authorities who have to

answer the case are called respondents. The cause title of a writ petition is usually a person versus a government or authority, for example, *Ram Kumar* v. *Union of India*, or *Ram Kumar* v. *State of Maharashtra*, or *Ram Kumar* v. *Municipal Corporation of Delhi*. (The Union of India is the official name of the Central government.) When the Court decides a matter in a writ, and determines whether the action of an authority was valid or not, it is said to have exercised the power of 'judicial review'.

3. **Public interest litigations** or PILs as they are often called are a kind of writ petition where the petitioner is not seeking relief just for himself or herself, but also for other persons or the public in general. PILs can be entertained by the High Courts and the Supreme Court. They are often criticized as being a vehicle for 'judicial overreach' – where the judiciary steps beyond its traditional function of deciding law, to creating and enforcing new law.

Judges are supposed to declare and apply the law that the people make through their legislators. In practice, judges often find themselves in a position to *make* the law; there is a very fine line between interpretation and creation. Sometimes, they are called upon to make decisions which are unpopular, and then we see some difficulties in implementing unpopular judicial decisions.

4.   **The hierarchy of courts:** At the very top is the Supreme Court, or Apex Court, which hears mostly appeals and writ petitions. Below that, each state (or sometimes a few states together) has a High court. The High Courts and the Supreme court are courts of record. They have wide powers, and can hear writ petitions. Their judgements bind the courts subordinate to them, and they can punish for contempt of courts. The cases before them should generally involve questions of law, such as whether Section 377 of the Indian Penal Code violates the Constitution or whether commercial speech is protected as free speech. Below the High Court level are the trial courts, which are further subdivided by seniority and by kind of court. Civil and criminal cases in our country by and large start in the trial courts. Trial courts take evidence, hear witnesses and determine questions of fact. For example, does Mr Ram Kumar own the house at 123 Main Street, or did Mr Ram Kumar kill Mr Shyam Kumar on the night of the First of November 2019? In practice, most cases involve a mixture of facts and of law.

5.   **Tribunals:** Some bodies of law are specialized and require different sets of procedure. Therefore, the law has

created separate tribunals for those kinds of cases. For environmental cases, one must go to the National Green Tribunal. For consumer cases, one goes to the Consumer Dispute Redressal Fora. The National Company Law Tribunal hear cases of corporate insolvency and shareholder disputes. Similarly, administrative law, labour laws, etc., also have specialized tribunals. From the tribunals one may appeal to the High Court or the Supreme Court as the case may be.

6. **Precedent:** The common law follows a principle called *stare decisis*, which is more commonly known as precedent – that where a position in the law has been decided earlier, unless there is good reason to differ, that position should be followed. The identical-looking books you see in floor-to-ceiling shelves in a lawyer's office, with years written on their spines, are reporters, which contain these precedents. With every year and every new case, new fact situations come up, and laws are applied to those situations by the court – from that comes case law. Very little of the law is explained by the sections you see in the acts; for example, Section 420 of the Indian Penal Code which says that cheating is a crime is under a hundred words long. The systematic exploration of how that section is applied, who

is guilty and who is not – what is or is not cheating – is laid down in the case law.

7. **Separation of powers:** Modern democracies such as ours have checks and balances built into them. One such is the separation of powers. We have three broad branches of government – the legislative, the executive and the judicial. The legislative branch consists of Parliament and state Legislative Assemblies. They are elected by the people and their primary power is to make law. The executive is the acting part of the government, which enforces the law and acts within the bounds of the law. The judicial branch is the part of the government which determines how the law is to be applied, and can judicially review the actions of the executive. This system of having three parts of government is designed to prevent the concentration of power in the hands of any one person or branch.

8. **Barristers, solicitors and briefings:** In England, there are two classes of lawyers: barristers and solicitors. Barristers argue cases in court, and solicitors prepare the papers and interact with the client. The solicitor briefs, or 'instructs' the barrister, and the barrister presents the case to the court, or conducts examination. In India, we follow this division more as a custom than as a rule, and lawyers are

free to draft, file and argue their own cases. However, there is a class of distinguished advocates whom the High Courts or the Supreme Court designates as senior advocates. Senior advocates are expected to have a wide breadth of expertise. They have usually practised law for at least twenty years before they are designated.

Hopefully these explanations will help you make sense of the chapters that follow, each of which is about a case or a pair of connected cases.

Anyone who wants to read these cases can search for them and find them easily. The judgements of our higher Courts are public documents and are intended to be read by anyone interested. But the judgements are the views of the judges, and are a top-down account of the battles before them. They are also usually dry accounts of facts and endless extracts of case law, and make for dull reading for the layperson.

The chapters that follow tell the stories of these cases from the perspective of a lawyer who argued them. This is what I was thinking, what I feared might happen, where I was taken aback, and how it felt. This is the view from the trenches.

I hope you enjoy it.

1

Is Commercial Speech Free Speech?

Tata Press v. *MTNL*

The life of a lawyer is unpredictable. There is no way to tell how a case may fall into your hands, or how long it may live. A case may go on for years and years, slowly climbing through the levels of the judiciary, while another may be withdrawn on the first day. You may have prepared for days and be bowled out first ball on a big case, and at other times an innocuous-seeming matter might open up questions of lasting importance. These ups and downs keep us lawyers on our toes.

One morning, I was walking through the corridors of the Supreme Court when I ran into my good friend Aspi Chinoy. Aspi is a very accomplished senior advocate who practises in Bombay, so it was a pleasant surprise to see him in Delhi. He is also somewhat unique among the legal fraternity because he takes a keen interest in yachting and sailing. I cannot think of another lawyer who is a sailor.

That morning, Aspi accosted me in the corridor and said he wanted me to come on board in an interesting matter. He had been representing Tata Press before the Bombay High Court, in a suit filed by Mahanagar Telephone Nigam Limited (MTNL), the government telephone company. Tata Press had been injuncted – restrained by an order of the Court – from publishing a Yellow Pages directory.

This may not mean a lot to some younger readers today, but before the Internet and mobile phones, landline phones were usually used alongside a telephone directory. If I wanted to look for the number of a restaurant or a shop, I would search through a directory, which was organized alphabetically and by categories, for the number. A telephone directory was essential for any home or business. MTNL argued that the Telegraph Rules of 1951 had decreed that no list of subscribers would be published without the permission of the government, and that the Yellow Pages brought out by Tata Press had flouted this restriction.

The suit had been filed by MTNL first before a trial court in Bombay, and the trial court had thrown it out on the basis that a directory of commercial entities, tradesmen, businesses, etc., was not the same thing as a list of subscribers, and therefore there was no reason to entertain the suit any further. MTNL then approached the Bombay High Court in appeal, and the Bombay High Court agreed with their argument that the list of tradesmen in the Yellow Pages was in fact a list of subscribers. Therefore, the government was entitled to stop Tata Press from publishing it.

Aspi Chinoy told me that Tata Press was committed to challenging the Bombay High Court's order before the Supreme Court in a special leave petition (SLP). An SLP is a kind of appeal to the Supreme Court from the orders of a lower court or tribunal, asking the Supreme Court to look into the matter because it contains a serious question of law. An appeal to the Supreme Court almost always starts life as an SLP.

Aspi asked me if it was worth taking on the bigger issues involved at a constitutional level, which they hadn't done so far. Would it make sense to additionally file a writ petition asking the Supreme Court if the fundamental rights of Tata Press had been violated? A writ petition is a very old and storied kind of remedy that has existed for the last five hundred years, where a higher court can enter into a question of the basic rights of a petitioner, and review the actions of government, and ask whether a constitutional provision has been violated by the law itself. Both the High Court and the Supreme Court can entertain writ petitions, and one of our weaknesses was that we had not already approached the High Court in writ and were going straight to the Supreme Court with the case.

My thinking was that the Tata Press should file both. In the SLP, they could ask the open question – whether they were violating the regulations in any way. That would be a question of interpretation – what do these regulations mean? Do my actions violate them? But in a writ petition, seeking enforcement of a fundamental right, we could ask a different sort of, and a much higher level of, question – do the regulations curtail my right to freedom of speech and expression under Article 19(1)(a), the article of our Constitution that guarantees us the freedom of speech?

At the heart of that would lie the greater question of whether commercial speech was entitled to protection under the Constitution. Does Article 19(1)(a) include within its broad scope commercial speech?

We discussed all this in the corridor that day, and

then Aspi went back to Bombay to discuss the matter with his solicitors. It was decided that I would lead the writ petition and Aspi would lead the appeal, and we would try both before the Supreme Court. The writ petition would be much wider – opening up the theoretical question.

Our strategy was to go for a two-pronged approach – the writ was a more adventurous remedy, for the larger constitutional question had never been raised before the High Court, and the Supreme Court could very well have chosen not to enter into it. If the bench was not interested, they could still be asked to consider the narrower question of correctness in the SLP.

The matter came up before one of the more interesting judges on the court – Justice Kuldeep Singh. Judges of course have different temperaments and approaches, and the fate of matters often hinges on their personalities. Kuldeep Singh was a robust, no-nonsense sort of judge, who wanted to get on with cases and dispose of them. He was a common-sense man, not the sort of judge to enthusiastically enter into philosophical arguments. We anticipated that he would veer towards discussing and disposing of the case on the narrower issue. Also, since the larger issue had not been raised in the Bombay High Court, we were already on a sticky wicket.

So in such a situation, what do you do? Do you start with the SLP, which is less likely to be dismissed? Or do you gamble on opening with the bigger issue since you have already lost in the High Court?

We decided to gamble on the bigger issue.

When the matter was called, I stood up before the Court and got straight to the trickiest part of our position. I admitted that we had not made this constitutional submission before the High Court. But I added that it was fully within the jurisdiction of the Supreme Court to entertain the writ petition arising out of the same set of facts. I put it to the bench boldly that it was time to revisit and reinterpret freedom of speech to include commercial speech. There was no reason for it to be an exception.

When I speak freely, whether in pursuit of my business, or partly in pursuit of my business and partly for non-commercial reasons, or just plainly to speak my mind, I am expressing myself – and that is the key aspect of freedom of speech and expression which is protected under the Constitution of India.

The argument for commercial speech was this. A

person who is selling his wares is talking about the qualities of his goods to attract customers. He is thus advertising something which is a commercial and not a charitable activity. But what difference does that make? Why should that stand in the way of his right to project his product as desirable to a customer? The same action can have two sides. You can express yourself positively about something. And this expression can also have a commercial motive. Self-expression cannot be limited to activities that are considered benevolent, or which are political or social.

Now there was already in place an authoritative judgement on commercial speech from a much larger bench, which would mean that it was binding on the present smaller bench. In 1960 the Supreme Court had found that commercial speech was not protectable under Article 19(1)(a). This was the case of *Hamdard Dawakhana* v. *Union of India*, where the constitutionality of the Drug and Magic Remedies Act was under scrutiny.

The Drugs and Magic Remedies (Objectionable Advertisement) Act of 1954 was a well-intentioned law. It prohibited advertising magical remedies. In a country which was at that time full of superstitions, and where the majority of the population was illiterate in any language, its aim was to preserve public health and bring accountability into advertising of these medicines.

In that instance, the Supreme Court decided that guarantee of freedom of speech was not the key factor and that commercial speech was not speech in the same sense as contemplated in Article 19(1)(a). In coming to that conclusion, they relied heavily on a 1942 American judgement, *Lewis J. Valentine* v. *F.J. Chrestensen*, where the Supreme Court of the United States held that advertising and handbills do not constitute protectable speech. Therefore, our Supreme Court followed suit and, in the context, their decision was correct.

Chrestensen had actually been reversed in its country of origin. In 1976 the Supreme Court of the United States had clarified that speech does not lose its constitutional protection merely because it is commercial in nature, in the case of *Virginia State Board of Pharmacy* v. *Virginia Citizens Consumer Council Inc.* Therefore, the historical basis on which the verdict of *Hamdard Dawakhana* had been decided had now weakened. I took this point and pushed hard on it, and this is what I think won us the case.

Justice Kuldeep Singh could not have overruled

Hamdard Dawakhana and said that it was bad law on its facts or findings, since his bench was much smaller than the *Hamdard* bench. But I argued that he could take a fresh look at the question in the present context, especially with *Chrestensen* having been overruled. It has to be said, however, that American judgements are not binding on our courts, but they can have persuasive value if their reasoning is sound.

Suppose I say that *Hamdard Dawakhana* is based solely and entirely on following *Chrestensen*. Now, *Chrestensen* has been overruled in the country of its origin. Is a court then compelled to follow a judgement which is based on overruled precedents? I was now relying on the new judgement which overrules *Chrestensen*. I was not saying that the Indian Supreme Court must follow the new foreign precedent, but only that it is at liberty to follow it or not follow it on its own merit.

This is where I must really tip my hat to Justice Kuldeep Singh. *Hamdard Dawakhana* was a five-judge constitutional bench, and he was presiding over a two-judge division bench. It would have been the easiest thing in the world for him to have said, 'I see your point, but I am bound to refer this to a bench which has the power to overturn a five-judge bench, which is a bench of seven judges.' In doing so, many years would have been lost.

To be honest, I don't agree with his approach. A system like ours is built on the framework of judicial discipline, precedent being followed, junior courts following senior courts, etc. While Justice Kuldeep Singh had been very bold in reopening the matter and right in this particular case, there is a larger systemic problem with his decision. Perhaps it would have been more correct for their lordships to have referred the case to a larger bench.

Of course, the matter was contested seriously. K.K. Venugopal and Arun Jaitley, both eminent seniors, whom it has always been a pleasure to oppose at the bar, appeared on the other side.

They said that the constitutional argument I was making was completely new at this stage. The High Court's job was to decide whether or not the Tata Press directory fell afoul of the current rule. They also argued that *Hamdard Dawakhana* was binding and that the Court was not sitting on the question of whether *Chrestensen* was good law.

I think Justice Kuldeep Singh was taken in by the

novelty of my case and arguments, and this tempted him to work around the procedural hobbles. The first argument I made was that apart from calling it commercial free speech, just for identification, there is no difference between 'valid' free speech and commercial speech, or personal and public speech, or praiseworthy and non-praiseworthy kinds of speech.

All speech is speech and is entitled to the protection under Article 19(1)(a). Some boundaries exist for what is protected and what is not. For example, defamation is an exception to the freedom of speech, as is harming public order, such as by shouting 'fire' in a crowded movie theatre. Therefore, there are laws against those categories of speech, and those laws are not struck down as violative of the Constitution. But within those limits, it is all still free speech in the same sense and to the same extent. Merely because I am using it to sell something, my speech does not lose the protection.

The law in the US took many steps to do what was done in India in *Tata Press*. First, they stopped at a halfway house protecting speech which, while commercial, has some political or social context, for example, advertising by Greenpeace. Then that false distinction between advertising with an agenda and advertising which was simply commercial and had no political or social agenda was eroded and then the US Supreme Court came to the stage of permitting pure commercial speech in *Virginia Board of Pharmacy*.

The differences between our Constitutions are often discussed. The US has a very strong law for the freedom of speech, without doubt, but it can be said, and I argued, that ours is more explicit.

This is the American First Amendment:

> *Congress shall make no law* respecting an establishment of religion, or prohibiting the free exercise thereof; or *abridging the freedom of speech, or of the press*; or the right of the people peaceably to assemble, and to petition the government for a redress of grievances.

> (emphasis added)

As you can see, the phrase from which all of American free speech law, which is the most robust in the world, emerges is 'Congress shall make no law ... abridging the freedom of speech, or of the press'.

The First Amendment is actually so wide that in the Constitution of India its contents fall under a number of different articles. But what is most remarkable is its absolute nature. In the phrase 'Congress shall make no law' is an absolute bar against curtailing these freedoms.

Our Constitution sets out a charter of freedoms and then a set of restrictions on those freedoms. The freedom of speech is guaranteed under Article 19(1)(a) and then curtailed under Article 19(2) by a set of 'reasonable restrictions'.

19. (1) All citizens shall have the right—
         (a) to freedom of speech and expression;
         .....

    (2) Nothing in sub-clause (a) of clause (1) shall affect the operation of any existing law, or prevent the State from making any law, in so far as such law imposes *reasonable restrictions* on the exercise of the right conferred by the said sub-clause in the interests of the sovereignty and integrity of India, the security of the State, friendly relations with foreign States, public order, decency or morality, or in relation to contempt of court, defamation or incitement to an offence.

                              (emphasis added)

Now, let us return to our case. I argued that the publishing of a directory by Tata Press could not be brought under one of the exceptions listed in Article 19(2). It was not a national security issue, not a public order issue, and there was no defamation involved. Then, in that case, on what basis was the freedom of speech being restricted?

Justice Kuldeep Singh, in the interest of the expansion of law and of Article 19(1)(a), took a bold step and did effectively change the law on the point. But, till date, nobody has questioned the ruling in *Tata Press*, or pushed it for reconsideration, on any grounds, including that it runs contrary to a larger bench. Why? Because an expanded reading of Article 19(1)(a) is in everyone's interest.

This has left a bit of a phantom in the system. The problem is that *Hamdard Dawakhana* is still good law; it has not been overruled. The Kuldeep Singh bench only really distinguished it, in the interest of expanding the rights under Article 19(1)(a) since 1960. It would be regressive for anyone to say that *Tata Press* should be reconsidered or reversed for that technical reason, and no court wants to go backwards.

A parallel can be drawn to the right to life under Article 21, which has made quantum advances in the last few decades as a reservoir of unenumerated, undefined rights. Article 21 merely says all persons shall have the right to life. By testing it in diverse circumstances, that right has grown into a full set of vivid living rights. For example, the right to life means that even pavement dwellers with no right to property cannot be evicted from public premises unless there is some plan for resettlement. The right to life has been read to mean the right to live in a clean and healthy environment, and the jurisprudence of environmental protection has been nurtured under that umbrella. It should be the same for Article 19(1)(a). These are the anchors of our democracy.

We had expanded the meaning of Article 19(1)(a) earlier as well. If you return to the text of the article above, do you see the word 'press' explicitly in the article anywhere? Obviously not. And yet press freedom is the most important kind of speech from a political perspective, and the courts have protected it as such. The Court has read the freedom of the press into Article 19(1)(a) since the very framing of the Constitution. If so, then why not for commercial speech. I knowingly painted it in those colours. I told the bench they could be seen as expanding a valuable freedom or curtailing it. I think that worked in my favour because a judge like

Kuldeep Singh would never want to be thought of as curtailing a freedom.

For the bold step I had invited the bench to take, the right judge was undoubtedly Kuldeep Singh. He was strong, vocal, hands-on and a bon vivant – a true sardar. Kuldeep Singh had a very impatient style, a sense of ambition and no time for the niceties of things in the courtroom. He liked to get to the heart of the matter and do effective justice. In the process, he was less than polite to counsel, sometimes even rude, which was fine given how counsels tend to wax eloquent even when there is nothing further to fight about. But he also had a great sense of humour. As an aside, let me tell you a story about his ability to take a joke.

G. Ramaswamy was a senior advocate who had come up the hard way. He was a real street fighter, and not born with a silver spoon in his mouth as so many of his contemporaries were. G. Ramaswamy and Kuldeep Singh had been Additional Solicitor Generals at the same time and so knew each other well. Kuldeep Singh went to the bench and G. Ramaswamy went on to become Attorney General. They both had in common their rough-and-ready, aggressive approach to the law – the insistence that arguments were not about technicalities but about getting the big picture right.

One day G. Ramaswamy was aggressively arguing a point which Kuldeep Singh was not inclined to accept. The judge was getting irritated with Ramaswamy while the counsel was exasperated by the judge's reluctance to see things his way. Justice Kuldeep Singh said, 'Mr Ramaswamy, how can we accept this point? Do you think we are fools?'

G. Ramaswamy retorted without a second's thought, 'My Lords, I don't know what to say. If I say yes, I will be guilty of contempt. If I say no, I will be guilty of perjury.'

It was, of course, brilliant. For a few seconds, Kuldeep Singh did not know what to do. Then he laughed for a whole minute – indeed the entire courtroom laughed for a long time. I find it hard to imagine our present judges having a similar exchange so sportingly.

Of course, we must remember that it was this same creativity with the law that led to Justice Kuldeep Singh's single-handed creation of the environmental law movement, in the M.C. Mehta cases of the 1980s and 1990s, where he took up PILs relating to environmental issues and passed orders directing major environmental preservation measures. He was the first green judge, and put into our body of law the principles that are now fundamental to environmental protection.

I think we would have reached the same result five years later, through the tortuous path of a larger bench. Nine out of ten judges would have given us the same result in those days, but they would have done it by a stale, sterile, pedantic path. Those were three words that Kuldeep Singh hated.

The Courts have long held that when you cut off the economic lifeline for freedom of speech, you are violating that right. This was tested in the 1950s and 1960s when the government sought to restrict the import of newsprint – and thereby made it more expensive to publish news. At that time the Courts stepped in to say that if you make it more expensive to speak, you are curtailing the freedom of speech and violating the Constitution.

Tata Press followed those principles and returned to the economic basis of the freedom of speech. The Court held:

Advertising is considered to be the cornerstone of our economic system. Low prices for consumers are dependent upon mass production, mass production is dependent upon volume sales, and volume sales are dependent upon advertising. Apart from the lifeline of the free economy in a democratic country, advertising can be viewed as the life blood of free media, paying most of the costs and thus making the media widely available. The newspaper industry obtains 60–80 per cent of its revenue from advertising. Advertising pays a large portion of the costs of supplying the public with newspaper. For a democratic press the advertising 'subsidy' is crucial. Without advertising, the resources available for expenditure on the 'news' would decline, which may lead to an erosion of quality and quantity. The cost of the 'news' to the public would increase, thereby restricting its 'democratic' availability.

The freedom guaranteed by *Tata Press* is more important now because there is so much more commercial speech. Our economy is more market-driven and more of what it puts out is commercial in nature. But it is also a concern that more of what is said, for better or worse, is determined by the commercial agenda. Look at our modern media landscape – the funding of enterprises controls their agendas explicitly. In this landscape, should the freedom of speech still include commercial free speech? I would say it should, because the limits imposed by Article 19(2) would still apply.

The other very interesting principle the Court relied on was that free speech is also a right embodied in the recipient or the audience of the speech. That is to say, not only is someone free to say what they want, but we all have a right to hear what is being said. The Court held:

> Examined from another angle, the public at large has a right to receive the 'Commercial speech'. Article (19)(1)(a) not only guarantees freedom of speech and expression, it also protects the rights of an individual to listen, read and receive the said speech. So far as the economic needs of a citizen are concerned, their fulfilment has to be guided by the information disseminated through the advertisements. The protection of Article 19(1)(a) is available to the speaker as well as to the recipient of the speech. The recipient of 'commercial speech' may be having much deeper interest in the advertisement than the businessman who is behind the publication. An advertisement giving information regarding a life saving drug may be of much more importance to general public than to the advertiser who may be having purely a trade consideration.

In the final analysis, I think the judgement in *Tata Press* has stood the test of time because it is actually correct. You have heard of hard cases making bad law, but here is an example of a hard case (hard given the circumstances of the judgement in *Hamdard Dawakhana*) making good law. By holding in our favour, the Court pushed forward the boundaries of Article 19(1)(a).

The facts, of course, change with time. Nobody uses telephone directories any more – young people under twenty-five may never have seen one. In those days telephone directories were considered a major advance in commercial advertising. Now we have a plethora of electronic advertising, all the services which promote and extend businesses, such as aggregators like Zomato. The creative expression of speech in those is also protected under Article 19(1)(a) following *Tata Press*.

We are also, of course, seeing new abuses which were unimaginable earlier. Newspapers every morning are given over to page after page of advertorial content, and newspaper editors know, as do we all, that it becomes impossible to distinguish between paid news and actual, unbiased news. The regulations for these malpractices have yet to be put in place. Paid news is a fraud on the public and, when it is passed off as the real thing, must be regulated. These are the new battles we are looking at, worldwide.

2

Who Watches the Watchmen?

D.K. Basu v. *State of West Bengal*

Imagine this: tonight, as you are having dinner with your family, there is a knock on the door. Two policemen enter and say you have to go with them. You go out of the door and are handcuffed, put into a police van and taken to the police station through the back entrance. You are taken to the basement and locked in a dark room. After eight hours, a man comes in and asks you about a conspiracy to assassinate the prime minister. You say you have never heard of such a thing.

Then, two constables tie you to a wall and beat you with sticks and electrocute you and ask you questions. You are untied and a piece of paper is put before you. You are told to sign it, and to avoid any further beatings, you sign it. Two days later, you are produced in a court, and you find that you have confessed to a conspiracy to murder the prime minister. Your signed confession is shown to you, and weapons mentioned in your confession are placed before you. Where do you start to protest your innocence?

For most of human history, throughout the twentieth century and even today, this nightmarish scenario has been completely possible. It is one of the oldest questions about law enforcement. As the Roman poet Juvenal asked in the second century AD, *Quis custodiet ispo custodies?* or Who will watch the watchmen? We all know the police exists to protect us from criminals and illegal activity, for example, violence. But what does one do when the violent criminal, the kidnapper, the murderer in some cases, is the policeman himself?

In the late 1980s, custodial violence and illegal arrests around India had reached a head. In a number of states, police forces had resorted to encounter killings to stop criminal activity. Terrorism in Punjab and states in the North-East, and then in Kashmir, had created an environment where law enforcement agencies felt they could not operate without bypassing the procedural safeguards in the law.

One may ask why this is a problem. At the end of the day, the people who are being arrested or tortured or killed, are they not the bad guys? The answer is that they may well be, or they may not, but the law does not and cannot operate like that.

The bones of our law are still very much English common law – the fine traditional system of justice developed over the past thousand years by the courts of England. One of the greatest principles of the common law is the presumption of innocence, that every man is innocent until proven guilty. This principle lies unquestionably at the root of our criminal law. The great English jurist William Blackstone famously wrote that it would be better to let ten guilty persons escape than for one innocent to suffer.

As a result, the basic process of criminal law is that the state has to prove the accused guilty, and until it does so in a court of law, the accused is deemed to be innocent. The burden on the state results in the creation of a number of safeguards. For example, confessions except when made voluntarily before a magistrate are to be disregarded. The idea is that confessions made to the police are often extracted by torture or coercion or inducement. A tortured person will admit to anything, whether guilty in the first place or not.

This idea – that no person shall be deprived of life or liberty without the due process of law – has run all the way down from the thirteenth century, when the Magna Carta was signed and the principles of limited government were first laid down by a reluctant King John in that famous meadow at Runnymede. Out of that guarantee springs the entire bouquet of our liberties – the right against self-incrimination, the right to a free and fair trial, etc.

In the twentieth century, with the creation of the United Nations and the international charter of human rights, the Convention against Torture and other instruments, these rules have truly acquired a universal status. These ideas are also embodied in the Indian Constitution.

But along the way, those principles have been tested, stretched and disregarded. State excess has been a historical fact, from the infamous medieval Star Chamber, where political trials were held in secret and acts which were not illegal were punished as if they had been, to politically motivated arrests in the present day across the world. Totalitarian states still use these methods. The question is how we strengthen our safeguards in the actual world – how we turn them from beautiful, high-minded words to instruments with which ordinary citizens can protect themselves.

If you enter a police station anywhere in India, you will notice one thing – a (more or less) prominently displayed set of guidelines of an accused person's rights in case of arrest. This is one of the major legacies of *D.K. Basu* v. *State of West Bengal*, the Supreme Court's landmark judgement against illegal and arbitrary arrests and custodial violence.

When the case began in 1986, I was a raw junior, who had been enrolled for only five years, but had practised much less since I had also been completing my PhD at Trinity College, Cambridge. Needless to say, experience is highly valued in the practice of law. With time comes a deeper knowledge of the law as well as an ability to read the court – to anticipate the thoughts of the judge and to approach his or her apprehensions with care and sensitivity. Litigation depends very much on the human touch, a judge's perception of a matter and of counsel.

The matter came up for the first time before Justice O. Chinnappa Reddy. I had earlier done a case before him for a poor man, Teja Singh, a former public servant, who was fighting the Union Territory of Chandigarh because he had been dispossessed of his house. He was an elderly, visibly ailing man, whose wife was also in poor health. I was representing him pro bono.

The Court ultimately could not give Teja Singh relief but there was genuine sympathy for his position, and they heard his case extensively. Justice Chinnappa Reddy heard me patiently even though he couldn't give me relief. This is probably why he thought of me when he read D.K. Basu's letter.

D.K. Basu himself was a retired judge of the Calcutta High Court. He had seen articles about custodial torture and deaths in the news. He addressed a letter to the Chief Justice of India, enclosing a number of articles about separate incidents, and asked why these violations of the law were being tolerated.

That letter was converted into a public interest litigation by the Supreme Court – in the law this has subsequently been called epistolary jurisdiction, a cause taken up by the court on the basis of a letter received by it. Epistolary jurisdiction is an excellent example of how wide the powers of the Supreme Court can be when it sees the need for it to exercise its jurisdiction.

Justice Chinnappa Reddy was very passionate about physical liberty, and he took an immediate interest in the matter. He appointed me amicus curiae, a legal term meaning 'friend of the court'. The appointment of an amicus curiae is a time-honoured practice where, when a problem requires research or impartial thinking and inputs, an advocate is appointed by the Court to look at the issue and address it without representing either side. At that nascent stage of my career, it was a great honour to be so appointed.

The issue of illegal arrests and custodial violence was a pan-India problem, and needed to be addressed by all twenty-five (at that time) states. The successive benches took interest in the matter, but there was very little meaningful progress for almost ten years. The delays were a result of the scale of the matter – since every state was a party, replies and data needed to be filed by each state.

Every time an application was moved, it would take nearly a year to ensure that all the parties, the respondent states, had been served and had filed their necessary responses. There would only be three or four hearings a year. As a junior lawyer, I couldn't force the pace much. We did a lot of hard work to glean data from the states, to prepare questionnaires and seek answers.

States were naturally reluctant to reveal bad truths about themselves, and dragged their feet as much as possible. The Court tried novel methods like confining hearings to only five states at a time, but the problem of unmanageability was unavoidable.

The state governments raised a few main arguments:

(a) They argued that the law already covers the violations raised. They pointed to the Code of Criminal Procedure which contains a number of safeguards; for example, enquiries had to be made into any allegations of custodial violence, and police who exceeded their mandate were to be punished.

The problem was that there were only two solutions for dealing with errant police officers – either to charge them with the crimes of assault or murder, or to initiate a disciplinary enquiry. From our data we had found that dismissals of policemen were very rare. What normally followed was a suspension. Almost never was there actual legal prosecution, which should follow as an automatic consequence. The more pertinent question was, what good did any of these remedies do to the victim?

(b) The second argument was that greater safeguards would lead to lawlessness as it would restrict meaningful investigation by the police.

This is what we call a scarecrow argument – it looks scary and important but there is no substance to it.

In no way are investigations hampered by safeguards against illegal arrest or custodial violence. The law supports extensive investigation and interrogation and preventive detention if necessary. But the law does not permit torture or 'third degree methods'. The answer to terrorism cannot be state terrorism.

(c) The third argument was that these safeguards are informally implemented in any case, and no orders were needed.

This argument should not prevent the Court from laying down minimum mandatory standards to ensure that the same standards are applied everywhere. Furthermore, the victims of such violations should be able to point to their rights in law and seek recourse if necessary.

Luckily, the case came to Justice A.S. Anand. Justice A.S. Anand was relatively more centrist than Justice Chinnappa Reddy, but he too was very keen on physical liberties. He breathed new life into the matter. By that time I was a senior advocate, and had been one since 1993, and could urge the matter more forcefully.

I told the Court that my problem was not in conceptualizing safeguards to apply after arrest. I gave the Court an extensive catalogue of existing safeguards and fresh safeguards we could apply. The difficulty was that in practice the police were routinely picking up people, beating or torturing them to extract information or to ensure compliance, and formally arresting them only later.

Since the formalities of arrest, paperwork and notifying the next of kin were only being done a few days later, none of the legal safeguards would apply till such time as arrest is formally recorded. In some circumstances, the victims of such mistreatment were even being medically treated before arrest. Therefore, at the time that you are produced before the magistrate, in accordance with the law, no mistreatment is taking place. Even now there is no real answer to this question.

On my recommendations, the Court laid down a set of procedural safeguards to be followed by all police forces across India and effectively made them law. In fact, by subsequent amendments to the Code of Criminal Procedure, 1973, these have come into legislation as well. These are, in short:

(1) The police personnel carrying out the arrest and handling the interrogation of the arrestee should bear

accurate, visible and clear identification and name tags with their designations. The particulars of all such police personnel who handle interrogation of the arrestee must be recorded in a register.

(2) That the police officer carrying out the arrest shall prepare a memo of arrest at the time of arrest and such a memo shall be attested by at least one witness who may be either a member of the family of the arrestee or a respectable person of the locality from where the arrest is made. It shall also be countersigned by the arrestee and shall contain the time and date of arrest.

(3) A person who has been arrested or detained and is being held in custody in a police station or interrogation centre or other lockup shall be entitled to have one friend or relative or other person known to him or having interest in his welfare being informed, as soon as practicable, that he has been arrested and is being detained at the particular place, unless the attesting witness of the memo of arrest is himself such a friend or a relative of the arrestee.

(4) The time, place of arrest and venue of custody of an arrestee must be notified by the police where the next friend or relative of the arrestee lives outside the district or town through the legal aid organization in the district

and the police station of the area concerned within a period of eight to twelve hours after the arrest.

(5) The person arrested must be made aware of this right to have someone informed of his arrest or detention as soon as he is put under arrest or is detained.

(6) An entry must be made in the diary at the place of detention regarding the arrest of the person which shall also disclose the name of the relative or next friend of the person who has been informed of the arrest and the names and particulars of the police officials in whose custody the arrestee is.

(7) The arrestee should, where he so requests, also be examined at the time of his arrest and major and minor injuries, if any present on his/her body, must be recorded at that time. The 'inspection memo' must be signed by both the arrestee and the police officer effecting the arrest and its copy provided to the arrestee.

(8) The arrestee should be subjected to medical examination by a trained doctor every forty-eight hours during his detention in custody.

(9) Copies of all the documents including the memo of arrest, referred to above, should be sent to the local magistrate for the record.

(10) The arrestee may be permitted to meet a lawyer during interrogation, though not throughout the interrogation.

(11) A police control room should be provided at all district and state headquarters, where information regarding the arrest and the place of custody of the arrestee shall be communicated by the officer carrying out the arrest, within 12 hours of effecting the arrest, and at the police control room it should be displayed on a conspicuous noticeboard.

The idea of these directions was to prevent the pitiable situation where the police would pick up a suspect and do what they wanted with him, with nobody knowing where he had been taken, whose custody he was in, whether some kind of writ had been filed, or who the relevant officers were. The police could no longer weaponize their silence.

The Supreme Court also went into the question of remedies for the victim. It would not give any meaningful satisfaction to a person who has been tortured and injured, or to the relatives of a person who has died in custody, to know that the culprits have been punished. How can their loss be made up to them?

The Court made it clear that the victims or the next of kin would be entitled to seek monetary compensation and that the compensation could be granted by a Court in a writ petition, as well as by the traditional method of filing a civil suit for damages. For many of the victims who were socio-economically disadvantaged compensation would be an important part of justice being done.

This was an important ruling because it functions as an exception to the rule of sovereign immunity, which says that the instruments of the state are not liable for any damage caused in the course of their duty. The law has now evolved the answer to that rule, which is that the actions which exceed a legal mandate are not protected by sovereign immunity.

That was how we closed the first *D.K. Basu* judgement in 1997. *D.K. Basu* is a good example of continuing supervision by the Court, as the petition stayed pending for follow-up and monitoring by the Court. Subsequent orders after 1997 have sought to expand the reach of the safeguards. The second set of safeguards, added by a judgement by Justice T.S. Thakur in 2015, tries to prevent violations by the police even before arrest, using tools like camera monitoring.

(1) The states of Delhi, Himachal Pradesh, Mizoram, Arunachal Pradesh, Meghalaya, Tripura and Nagaland were directed to set up State Human Rights Commissions (SHRCs). All vacancies for the posts on the SHRC wherever they existed were to be filled up by the state governments concerned within a period of three months from the vacancy.

(2) The state governments were to take appropriate action for setting up/specifying human rights Courts.

(3) The state governments were to take steps to install CCTV cameras in all the prisons in their respective states, if possible in a phased manner depending upon the incidents of human rights violations reported in such stations.

(4) The state governments were to consider appointment of non-official visitors to prisons and police stations under the relevant provisions of the act wherever they exist in the jail manuals or the relevant rules and regulations.

(5) The state governments were to launch in all cases where an enquiry establishes culpability of the persons in whose custody the victim has suffered death or injury an appropriate prosecution for the commission of offences disclosed by such enquiry report and/or investigation in accordance with law.

(6) The state governments were to consider deployment
of at least two women constables in each police station
wherever such deployment is considered necessary
based on the number of women taken for custodial
interrogation or interrogation for other purposes over
the past two years.

When regular monitoring by the Supreme Court
became impractical, the National Human Rights
Commission (NHRC) was brought in to monitor the
issue, and the NHRC and the SHRCs were directed to
give regular reports. At that point we discovered that
50 per cent of the states did not even have an SHRC
in place. The states were then directed to set up SHRCs
and get them running. I sometimes joke that as a result
I am responsible for providing sinecures to a number
of retired judges.

Now every police station displays the guidelines and
there has been some cultural change. Having CCTV
cameras in police stations, for example, ensures real-
time accountability. It is always possible for the CCTV
camera to be pointed the wrong way, of course, but it is
a beginning and it is making a difference.

The insertion of so much of the language from the judgements into the Code of Criminal Procedure is also a huge step – from judge-made law in case law to black-letter code in legislation. We have learnt over the years that it is one thing for lawyers and the court to know what the law means, but it is equally effective to have the law in the actual legislation, which the police and laypeople read as well.

As I write this, it is hard not to look at cases covered by the media which look suspiciously like extrajudicial killings, such as in the Hyderabad rape case. The fact is our commitment to fair and complete justice is tested by extreme provocations like the horrific rape and murders of Nirbhaya in Delhi, Priyanka Reddy in Hyderabad and of the victim in Unnao. But to preserve a rule-following society, this is when we must be most scrupulous to preserve the safeguards of the law – to ensure fairness and justice to all. We must follow the principle of 'dharmo rakshati rakshitah', that the law will protect those who protect the law. No good is done by extrajudicial executions and mob justice. We will now never know whether the murdered accused were truly guilty or whether they were innocent and the truly guilty have gone free and may commit further crimes.

Our record on prosecutions for custodial deaths and extrajudicial killings is still shameful. For every hundred custodial deaths there have only been a few dozen prosecutions and convictions almost never take place.

While we still have many miles to go, it has now become that much harder for true abuse of the process to exist. The police will still exceed authority and act rashly, but now the policeman must look twenty times instead of twice as he would have earlier. That culture of impunity has been breached and the widespread excesses of the 1980s are unlikely to be repeated. We must take satisfaction by looking at where we started and where we are today.

~

A similar case where I had the opportunity to assist the Court with an issue of grave public interest was *In Re Death of 25 Chained Inmates in Asylum Fire in Tamil Nadu* in 2002. In a horrifying incident at the Moideen Badusha Mental Home at Erwadi in Tamil Nadu in August 2001, a fire had broken out at a mental asylum. Twenty-eight inmates had died because they were chained to their beds and could not free themselves to escape. The Moideen Badusha Mental Home was affiliated to a local dargah, where the mentally ill were often taken by their relatives. The treatments included prayer as well as beatings and canings to drive away 'demons' inside the patients.

This medieval approach to the treatment of the mentally ill shocked the Supreme Court, which took up the matter on its own motion after seeing reports in national dailies. I was appointed amicus in 2001 by Justice A.S. Anand.

While the Mental Health Act of 1987 had been passed by the legislature in 1987, it had not been implemented by the Central government and state governments in a serious fashion. As a result, a slew of unlicensed and unregulated institutions carrying out all kinds of mental health treatments, some with little or no connection to medical science or psychiatry, were operating.

On my suggestion, a set of reports on the implementation of the Mental Health Act, 1987, were sought from the state governments including checking whether the mental health hospitals being privately run were properly licensed, and if not, the local police was to be charged with shifting the patients to a government-run hospital. Each state was also directed to set up at least one fully fledged mental health hospital and to undertake awareness campaigns about mental health to ensure patients were being sent to proper care centres and not being abandoned at temples or dargahs as was common practice.

Since then, the recommendations made by me to the Court in mental health matters have been incorporated into case law and have also passed into the statute book. The new Mental Health Act of 2017 is thoroughly humane, progressive and largely up to the standards globally embraced for the treatment of those suffering from mental health issues.

When I look at these cases, and similar cases which are reported in the newspapers, I think what it would be like to live in a society which genuinely respects human life. The kinds of horrors that are visited upon the marginalized and oppressed in these systems need to be probed again and again. We must be vigilant. It is the only way our society can honour its constitutional guarantees of a decent life for all.

3

The Sabarimala Case

Women in the Temple

Here is one vision:

In the dense hilly forests of Kerala, inside a tiger reserve, there is an ancient temple, dedicated to Lord Ayyappa. It has sat in the misty forests for at least a thousand years – its origins are lost in myth and antiquity.

Every year there are only a few days when it is possible to visit the temple, and on those few days millions of worshippers stand in line. In the morning, a line of pilgrims starts from the last forest camp for the temple. This is the end of a journey which has taken them days, or even months.

Traditionally, a man who wishes to visit the temple at Sabarimala must take a sacred vow, a *vratham*, which requires him to undergo forty-one days of austerities.

The vratham is designed to inculcate in the worshipper a sense of brahmacharya, no matter what stage of life he may be at, and to purify his body and mind.

As part of the vratham, for forty-one days the worshipper eats only one meal a day, which is to be vegetarian – he forswears meat, alcohol, cigarettes and tamasic food. He cooks his own food and visits a temple every day. Because he is now observing the life of a brahmachari, he is celibate and forsakes physical relations with his spouse (if he has one) and otherwise does not keep the company of women.

In his belief system, to be around women of reproductive age is to be distracted from the vow of brahmacharya. To accomplish this, he lives in a separate room if possible. Even his dress code changes, and he wears a blue or black mundu and vest, and goes barefoot. He does not cut his hair or clip his nails.

After these forty-one days, the pilgrim takes the *irumudikettu*, which is a package of offerings, and starts the pilgrimage to the temple. Some start from as far away as 60 kilometres and some approach from much closer, but when they embark, they cover some part of the ancient trail, entering the hills of Sabarimala and crossing the river Pampa.

At the temple, they come to the eighteen steps or the *pathinettu thripadikkal*, the last steps to the temple. According to tradition, only those who have observed the penances of the vratham or who are carrying the irumudikettu may climb the final eighteen steps to the temple.

The pilgrim is retracing a journey taken for thousands of years, and first taken by the very god he has come to worship – Lord Ayyappa. According to legend, Ayyappa is a syncretic deity, the son of Shiva and Vishnu in his female form as Mohini.

He was found by the king of Pandalam as a radiant infant on the banks of the river Pampa, wearing a set of beads ('mani') around his neck. The king of Pandalam, instantly enamoured and awestruck by the child, adopted him and called him Manikandan. Manikandan's feats as a child and an adolescent convinced the king and others of his divine origin. One day, Manikandan shot an arrow into the forest and told the king that a temple should be built where the arrow was found. That arrow fell at what is now Sabarimala.

Manikandan then himself undertook the forty-one-day vratham and took the ancient path to the temple at Sabarimala, and merged with the idol there, and became known as Lord Ayyappa. Since then, to believers, he has resided there, and every pilgrimage to the temple is a retracing of the journey of Manikandan, who became Lord Ayyappa.

As Lord Ayyappa was the son of two male gods, Shiva and Vishnu (as Mohini), he is a hypermasculine deity, and eternally celibate – *naishtik brahmachari*. This celibacy extends to giving up the company of women and even thoughts of women. When the pilgrim replicates the deity's journey, he seeks the same state of brahmacharya. This is why women who are between ten years and fifty years of age are not permitted to visit the temple at Sabarimala – their presence interferes with the completely celibate practice of the pilgrims who have held to their vow.

But that's only one perspective.

In 2006 what was presented to the Supreme Court in the case of *Indian Young Lawyers Association & Ors.* v. *State of Kerala & Ors.* was another perspective, and one which clashed directly with the first. This came from the Ayyappa devotees who were women between ten and fifty years of age.

Why were they not permitted into the temple? Could such an exclusion ever be justified in an equal society?

Why was the burden of the celibacy of the male pilgrims being heaped upon their heads?

Most great constitutional matters involve competing interests, a clash of rights. In balancing between two legitimate rights, something valuable is often lost. In the case of Sabarimala, we were looking at the deep clash between the rights of two classes of believers. It was also a clash between a very appealing broad-brush argument and a finely nuanced legal position.

Let us take a step back and think about how our Constitution, and our polity, views religion. We know that India is still a very religious country, most people profess a religion and a great number of those are deeply observant. Therefore, a fine balance must be engineered between permitting people the free exercise of their faith and ensuring that their faith does not interfere with the law and order, with our secular society and, equally importantly, with the faith of other people.

First, let us look at the articles of the Constitution which are relevant.

Article 14. The State shall not deny to any person equality before the law or the equal protection of the laws within the territory of India.

Article 14 is the most important source for equal treatment in our Constitution. It lays a basis for the principle of equality, and Articles 15 and 16 elaborate on how equality works in some circumstances, that is, in education and jobs. Article 14 states that equality is about treating 'equals equally, and unequals unequally in such a way as to restore or bring about equality'.

So, for example, reservations are constitutionally valid in education, for Scheduled Castes or Scheduled Tribes, because due to poverty, caste bias and other structural factors, they have historically not had access to good education. A reserved category is thus necessary for them to level the playing field. Paradoxical as it may sound, sometimes to treat two people equitably, we have to treat them differently.

To make such a discrimination, every case must meet two tests. First, that the discrimination is a sensible one for a good reason – this is called the test of intelligible differentia. Second, that there is a rational nexus, or connection, between the good which is sought to be achieved and the categorization which is made. In the case of reservation at a college, the factor of intelligible differentia is met by the fact that only those communities are given reservation which have been historically underprivileged. The rational nexus is that this differentiation helps colleges admit students more equitably.

Turning to religion in particular, our Constitution is clear that India is a secular country and that the state will not interfere in religious belief and practice.

Article 25. (1) Subject to *public order, morality and health* and to the other provisions of this Part, all persons are equally entitled to freedom of conscience and the right freely to profess, *practise* and propagate religion.

(2) Nothing in this article shall affect the operation of any existing law or prevent the State from making any law –

(a) regulating or restricting any economic, financial, political or other secular activity which may be associated with religious practice;

(b) providing for social welfare and reform or the throwing open of Hindu religious institutions of a public character to all classes and sections of Hindus.

(emphasis added)

Article 25 sets out the broad religious freedoms that every person in India is entitled to – they are free to practise their religion, and this practice includes rituals and the traditions of dress, diet, worship, travel, performance, etc. – all the performative parts of religion. If a law is made which interferes with those, it has to be tested against constitutional protection. However, a person's religious freedoms cannot offend public order, morality or health. My religion cannot tell me to go out and throw stones at a non-believer, and if it does, that practice can be outlawed and will not have constitutional protection.

Article 25(2)(a) sets out what lies beyond the realm of the state. It cannot enter into the private belief or practice of an individual, but when religion has a political or economic manifestation, it can be regulated by the state. So, for example, if a temple starts to sell a food product, then food packaging and labelling laws would apply.

Article 25(2)(b) is very interesting because it shows the vision and intent of the early Indian state. This sub-clause expressly allowed those laws which were passed to open up temples to believers of all castes. When the Constitution did away with untouchability in 1950, to give effect to that, the necessary acts for temple reform had to be passed ensuring that no person was turned away from a temple on the basis of caste – the historical barriers on entry into temples for certain castes were torn down. Discrimination on a caste basis can never be defended.

> Article 26. Subject to public order, morality and health, every *religious denomination* or any section thereof shall have the right –
> (a) to establish and maintain institutions for religious and charitable purposes;
> (b) *to manage its own affairs in matters of religion;*
> (c) to own and acquire movable and immovable property; and
> (d) to administer such property in accordance with law.
> (emphasis added)

Now this is interesting! In Article 14 or Article 25 we saw that the rights to believe, practise and propagate are all individual rights, which belong to each person. But Article 26 talks about the rights of a religious denomination – what is that?

Our courts have sat over the last seventy years to work out tests for that. There must be some objective measure of what a denomination is or is not, to distinguish between what has always been a tradition or practice and what may be created today by someone to carry out a practice. Broadly, in order to be a denomination, there are three conditions:

(1) It must be a collection of individuals who have a system of beliefs or doctrines professed by them, that is, a common faith;
(2) They must have a common organization; and
(3) They must have a distinct public identity, conveyed by a distinctive name.

A religious denomination or group has a right to open institutions and manage their own affairs in accordance with their internal principles, subject to certain very high thresholds. Much of what we see in our daily lives in the realm of religion reflects this right.

The opening and closing hours that the law allows to shops and offices do not bind temples, for example. It is on this group imagination of religion that a lot of India's cultural practices work – for example, the date when an Eid falls is dependent on the leader of a denomination sighting the moon. It is not decided by an individual Muslim.

In theory, even assuming there was no Article 26, there would be a group right in religion constitutionally. People have a right to believe. They also have a right to form groups, to speak freely, to move about freely. Those rights naturally lead to a group right in religion.

Now let us test these principles against the facts in the Sabarimala case. Male pilgrims have a right to worship and to practise as they see fit. Women devotees of Lord Ayyappa also have a right to worship and to practise as they see fit. Further, if the priests of the temple and the pilgrims are to be called a denomination, they too have a right to manage their own affairs as they see fit. Between the individual right to worship of those women who wish to enter the Sabarimala temple and the group right of the Ayyappa priests and pilgrims there is a clash.

This was framed in Kerala's laws as a sort of negative permission, in that the Kerala Hindu Places of Public Worship (Authorisation of Entry) Rules, 1965, contained Rule 3(b) which read that 'women at such time during which they are not by custom and usage allowed to enter a place of public worship' would *not* be entitled to offer worship or enter such premises. Therefore, the law did not exclude the women in question, but permitted the temple to exclude them if it was custom or usage to do so.

I was engaged in the matter by the Travancore Devaswom Board, which was the trust which managed the temple, and so I was representing the priests, the pilgrims and the right to exclude women of certain ages from the temple.

The striking aspect about the case was that the petitioners were an association of lawyers filing in public interest on behalf of the women who were allegedly aggrieved.

The women themselves, that is, women between ten and fifty years of age who wanted to go to Sabarimala, never came forward. On the other hand, there were lakhs of women who said the opposite. They gave their affidavits to that effect.

Second, as this was a PIL filed directly before the Supreme Court, there was no trial or determination of whether certain facts were true or false. The problem with this method is that it forces the court to rely on affidavits – which are first-person accounts.

When a fact is found in a proper trial, such as after examining a number of experts and going through ancient documents, whether a practice is essential to a religion or not, or whether a group is a 'denomination', then a better determination of rights can be made. In all the earlier cases which came to the Court about the determination of essential religious practices, there was a trial, and there was a basis for reaching the conclusions the Court reached.

In a question of this sort, the persons cast as respondents, who may lose rights, have also lost access to the many levels of adjudication and appeal that would normally come before the Supreme Court heard the matter.

The petitioners argued on three grounds. These were:

(1) On Article 14, that there was inequality since there was discrimination on the basis of being a certain gender.
(2) On Article 17, that the exclusion was a form of untouchability which was expressly forbidden by the Constitution.
(3) On grounds of Articles 25 and 26, saying that the practice of exclusion did not legally qualify as an essential religious practice of a denomination.

The first two I think we can deal with easily.

As I wrote earlier, to allow for exceptions to Article 14, any case has to pass two tests.

Applying that test, the discrimination here is not against all women, but only women between ten and fifty years of age when they may have menses, and the rational nexus with the object of the discrimination is that the temple at Sabarimala contains the Naishtik Brahmachari avatar of Ayyappa, and the eternal celibate nature of the deity abjures all relations with women who are of an age when they are sexually mature.

The first test is that the discrimination is a sensible one for a good reason – or the test of intelligible differentia. The second is that there is a rational nexus, or connection with the good which is sought to be achieved.

The discrimination is inherently entwined with the nature of the deity. The legitimate object is to permit that religious denomination the freedom to manage its own affairs in line with its essential beliefs. The exclusion is only practised at the temple at Sabarimala – and not in any of the other fifteen hundred Ayyappa temples across India. There are in fact eight temples to Lord Ayyappa in the NCR alone, all of which admit women. The reason is simple – the Sabarimala temple is the sole one where the deity is in his avatar as a naishtik brahmachari. The exclusion of women there is inextricably intertwined with the nature and identity of the deity – the only one of this kind in the entire world.

The petitioners further argued that there was no difference between a woman who was of ages ten to fifty and any other woman, and that a physiological difference such as menstruation was not a fair differentiating factor.

The Article 17 argument was a red herring – untouchability in the Constitution means only untouchability as a question of caste or birth. There is no question of that being applied to women in any sense as a class. The horror that is untouchability was so offensive to the framers of the Constitution that they devoted a full article to it – and it was clear that their intention was never to cast a net so wide that it would dilute the focus from untouchability arising by caste or birth and apply to anything else. However, for precisely that reason, it is the sort of argument which is sometimes superficially attractive to judges. The bar at Sabarimala was not caste-based – that could never have been defended.

The matter here was to turn on the old question of essential religious practices.

The tests of what makes a practice an essential religious practice were conceptualized by the Supreme

Court in the early years of the Indian republic to determine which practices could be protected from legislation and which could not.

For example, in the famous case of the Anand Margis, the commissioner of police in Calcutta banned them by an order from carrying out their tandava dance, in which they would in public carry trishuls and other weapons and human skulls. In law, he could not have banned them if it were an essential religious practice, unless it was also a violation of public order. In that particular case, the carrying of the trishuls and weapons was found not to be an essential religious practice, so the ban was held to be valid.

Similarly, in the case of the Dawoodi Bohras of Bombay, a law was passed preventing any excommunications, and following the act, an excommunicated Dawoodi Bohra claimed before the Supreme Court that he had a right to be part of the community and could not be excommunicated. The community claimed a right to excommunicate. The Court tested the right and found ecommunication to be an essential religious practice for Dawoodi Bohras. Therefore, the law preventing excommunication was invalidated.

There is a problem here which you, the reader, may have already stumbled on – how does a secular court determine the importance of a religious practice? After all, judges are not usually believers of whatever denomination they are trying to understand. Faith is by definition irrational. Whether a god stood upon a point or a prophet uttered certain words is something that is absolutely held to be true by a believer. To anyone who is not a believer, it is no more than a fanciful story.

But how does a secular judge, sitting over a modern constitution, using tools evolved by English common law, determine which part of a thousand-year-old practice is 'essential'? It forces a judge to become a theologian for a day, and scholars have long criticized this development of the law, but it is what we must work with.

I argued that the test the Court was bound to apply was this:

(1) Was the practice of excluding women aged ten to fifty a religious practice by nature? Did it have its roots in the belief system?

(2) Was it an essential religious practice for that denomination of believers?

(3) Did it otherwise offend public order, morality or health?

This test is part subjective and part objective. For the first part, to determine essentiality, we must step into the shoes of the believer. To some extent, historical documents, archaeological evidence and other forms of evidence can help us – but telling the difference between an inessential and essential part of religious practice is still a subjective determination. The second part, whether something offends public order or morality or health, is objectively determinable by the court.

For the devotees of Lord Ayyappa at Sabarimala, their deity was the Naishtik Brahmachari avatar of Ayyappa. Of the more than fifteen hundred temples in India to Lord Ayyappa, this was the only one devoted to the Naishtik Brahmachari avatar, and therefore the only one to exclude women between those ages. I may not be a believer, you may not be a believer, but the law expects judges to look at what the believer believes.

Barring a few exceptions, from the depths of recorded history, at Sabarimala, Lord Ayyappa was worshipped in this form. Believers in that avatar have a common set of beliefs and practices – the vratham, the penances, the celibacy for forty-one days, the pilgrimage through the forest. They have a common organization, a priesthood, a dress code, days when the temple can be visited. The *thantri*, the head priest of the temple, was represented before the Supreme Court as well. The believers have a name – they are commonly called Ayyappas. I argued that, therefore, they are in the eyes of the court a religious denomination, and to them this practice of exclusion is sacred.

The petitioners' argument about religious denomination was also a strong one. It is one thing, they argued, for a group to have an identity which is the same across all places of worship. But every temple cannot be permitted to make its own denomination; that would undo the basis of the constitutional reasoning. It is a good argument – can one temple be considered significant enough to create an essential religious practice? I would argue in the case of Sabarimala, or Tirupati, it can be.

Then there is the question of burden of proof. In legal proceedings, the person who files the case, as a plaintiff in a civil case, a petitioner in a writ petition or a prosecution in a criminal matter, must prove his case and convince the court before the other side has to defend themselves.

The burden of proof, once a claim to an essential religious practice is made, ought to have rested on the petitioners to show from evidence that there was no religious denomination or essential religious practice, that is, that there were no constitutional protections. A problem I often find in PILs is that an unfair burden is cast upon the respondents to justify practices that have not even convincingly been attacked. Of the exceptions none were argued by the petitioners, and for good reason.

There is no argument of public order – the exclusion is not causing riots. There is no issue of health – nobody is suffering any health issues as a result of the pilgrimages. And there is no question of morality – which is an exception that is not immediately clear but which has been understood to be something as offensive to human nature as cannibalism, something no society can condone. There is also no physical or mental harm caused to any person.

Once we enter the domain of faith, I argued, the only really important thing is knowing what the believer believes. I asked the Court a common-sense question – assume you are allowed to go to a temple, are you allowed to do all forms of worship at all times?

In the Vallabhacharya temple, can you visit during the *shayya kal* of the god? The deity is deemed to be sleeping during that particular time. Can you wake up the deity at one o'clock at night instead of three o'clock when the *suprabhat* starts in Tirumala? Can you do an aarti at 2 p.m. instead of 6 p.m.? These are practices of the people at those temples, and their legitimacy emanates from what they mean to the people who go there.

Another point that I argued which also made an impact was the uncomfortable question of whether women are allowed in temples during menses. Obviously, nobody asks a woman at a temple whether she is on her periods. There is a concept of purity involved and there is an unspoken restriction which many Hindu women obey as self-imposed discipline. A similar concept of purity exists in other religions as well, in Judaism and in Islam and in most of the older religions. For that matter, many Sunni mosques in India do not customarily permit the entry of women. It may not be rational or sensible to all of us today, but it is what the believer believes.

Which leads us back to the question of whose rights are being sought here. Lakhs of women who are believers went on record saying that while they are Ayyappa believers, they would not go to Sabarimala. Their menfolk would go and their mothers over the age of fifty would go, but they would not – their belief system proscribed it. The women who were represented by the petitioners were in a minority. All of them were entitled to visit more than a thousand Ayyappa temples – just not the one at Sabarimala.

In matters of religion, we open a can of worms when we question practices logically. Is it regressive to bar women from entering a place? Almost certainly. But religion is by nature opposed to progressive belief. If a thing was universally, scientifically, objectively ascertainable, we would not need religion to tell us of that thing. But the realm of religion, mystical, regressive, primitive, call it what you will, is protected by our Constitution. It was on this principle – the freedom to decide one's own beliefs – that we rested our case.

We lost the case. The Supreme Court decided in their landmark decision to go against us, and in favour of the petitioners. The matter was decided 4:1, where Justices Dipak Misra, A.M. Khanwilkar, R.F. Nariman and D.Y. Chandrachud were in favour and Justice Indu Malhotra dissented.

Chief Justice Dipak Misra, writing for himself and Justice Khanwilkar, came to the conclusion that the exclusionary practice protected by Rule 3(b) of the Kerala Act violated the right of Hindu women to freely practice their religion under Article 25, and that the exclusion was not an essential religious practice. His opinion hinged on a reading of the right under Article 25 of the individual's religious freedom as being paramount and which cannot be restricted by gender or physiological factors specific to women. In his judgement, he did not really deal with the rights of the denomination or of essentiality – as far as he was concerned, the only question was a fundamental one of equality.

Justice R.F. Nariman wrote that there was no basis for the worshippers at the Sabarimala temple being defined as a denomination because men of other faiths, Hindus of all kinds, and Muslims and Christians, also visit it, as they do all the other Ayyappa temples. He also found that there was no one distinct name for the denomination. Therefore, in his view, Article 26 protections were not available to the respondents.

Justice D.Y. Chandrachud agreed with both of the above views but expanded further on a concept called 'constitutional morality' which he read to believe that the Constitution has a certain moral framework of fairness, equality and freedom built into it which permits the

Court to interpret the law in such a way as to amplify those virtues.

He also interpreted Article 17 of the Constitution, arguing that questions of purity or pollution constituted a form of untouchability. Justice Chandrachud followed on some of the similar principles he had enunciated in *Navtej Johar* v. *Union of India*, the Section 377 case, that is, where same-sex intercourse was decriminalized.

Justice Indu Malhotra dissented from the majority. She held the worshippers of Sabarimala to be a denomination, finding that the exclusion was inherently connected to the nature of the deity and therefore an essential religious practice. She also argued that there was no question of Article 17 being expanded beyond caste, and that the issues of essential religious practices were for the religious community in question to decide.

Afterwards, Justice Malhotra's dissent was heavily criticized in the press. It was very disappointing to see the negative reaction to Justice Indu Malhotra's dissent merely because she was a woman. To my mind, her opinion is by far the most legally sound, and not merely because it was in our favour.

Justice Chandrachud's opinion enters the question of what should and should not be permitted in religious

80

practice, and in introducing the idea of 'constitutional morality' may well have opened an unmanageable door to an ocean of subjectivity. Constitutional morality in the hands of the wrong judges can mean whatever they need it to mean.

There is a saying in English law that 'equity is as long as the chancellor's foot', which refers to a time that English courts of equity were different from formal courts of law, and although the law was a certain thing, leaving things to the conscience of one person, that is, the chancellor, was not. Therefore, the saying goes, if we want to know how long a foot is, and it was dependent on the chancellor, one chancellor might have a long foot, and another a short foot, and similarly, depending on who was sitting in the chair or how he felt on a given day, the result might be different. Constitutional morality is such a 'chancellor's foot'. It is an unruly horse and the very high degree of dexterity of judicial riders required to apply it fairly and correctly is a rare exception rather than the usual rule.

The widespread application of this uncertain doctrine, this unruly horse that is constitutional morality, is dangerous. Equality and fairness as overriding virtues, in the wrong hands, can become instruments of tyranny and bias. There is a reason the law is technical and rule-based. Today, we have good and learned judges like Justice Chandrachud, but I shudder to imagine the same creative licence in the hands of a weak, confused or less intellectually equipped judge.

I also agree with Justice Malhotra that the PIL is the wrong forum for questions like these. In earlier times, these questions came to the Court after trials, where questions of fact had been laid to rest. Now, a judge is free to scan through affidavits and reach a conclusion as to whether, for example, a practice is an essential religious practice. Further, the burden of proof gets inverted and loaded upon the respondent in such a PIL. As a result, judges can cherry-pick what to rely on. Abandoning the rules of procedure can often result in judges erring – such rules are there to guide the judicial mind to the right answer.

Let us be honest. With Sabarimala, the Court was under tremendous pressure from the media. There was no way to give another verdict without being painted as regressive. The press set standards for the Court, and I believe this was definitely a factor in the way the Court ruled.

We all mind losing cases, but at the end of the

day, what matters to a lawyer is that he or she made a complete and credible argument, which I feel we did. The Court could have gone in our favour, and I feel if it had been guided by the past law correctly, it should have.

In the aftermath of the judgement, there were massive protests in Kerala, and the way to the temple was barricaded by thousands of devotees. Two women ultimately managed to enter the temple under heavy police escort. As a result, there were riots in the state which had to be controlled by police action. Afterwards, priests at the temple carried out a purification ritual. It is very hard to change people's minds by passing judgements. Of course, once the law has been settled, it must be followed.

A large number of review petitions challenging the judgement of the Supreme Court were filed. Typically, review petitions, especially where judgements by such large benches are to be considered, are seldom allowed. I appeared in the review also and pointed out some of the problems with the majority view in the judgement.

The review petitions were allowed by the Supreme Court in late 2019, stating that since similar issues had arisen in a number of cases, across faiths, the questions in Sabarimala ought to be decided by a larger bench.

The question is now pending before a nine-judge bench, ironically being heard when this book is going to press.

Though I appear to have temporarily succeeded by this second judgement, I hope it is finally heard and decided soon. In a matter this contentious, where one knows that people will react in such a fashion, it would be the right thing for the larger bench to hear the matter as quickly as possible and close the matter one way or another. It is now ongoing before a nine-judge bench where I again happen to be appearing – a third time. Hopefully, a quietus on such important legal issues will come soon.

4

Flying High

Naveen Jindal v. *Union of India*

National flags and national anthems are emotional issues. We grow up with them, in school as children, on national holidays, at times of struggle or of strife. India has been to war a few times in my lifetime, and we have seen our fellow citizens fight and die for the flag. That makes the flag much more than a piece of cloth for me. It is a rich and powerful symbol of the founding and strength of our nation. It may not be that way for children today – perhaps the historical weight of the flag is not as great for them as it is for those of my generation.

Yet, as one who loves the flag and respects it, until fifteen years ago, I was in the odd position of being forbidden by law from flying it. There are countries across the world where the flag is fairly freely used. In the United States or in Brazil, for example, it can be used as clothing, as decoration, or for any number of purposes. It can, unacceptably to me, even be burnt. That is not so in India.

I knew Naveen Jindal socially, from before either of us was a member of Parliament. I have found him to be an unusual industrialist in the way he has organized his life: devoting one-third of his time each to industry, politics and to keeping fit – he is a keen polo player and an avid marksman. Somewhere along the line, he had also acquired a passion for our flag.

Once when he was flying the flag at one of his Raigarh factories, he was stopped from doing so and prosecuted by the government for violation of the Flag Code. This led to the first round of the case, which I did not take part in. Naveen Jindal filed a writ petition against the Union of India in the Delhi High Court challenging the Flag Code on a number of grounds. It was argued before Justice D.P. Wadhwa and Naveen Jindal was represented by Shanti Bhushan.

The flying of the flag in India was governed by the National Emblems (Prevention of Improper Use) Act, 1950, which prevents the improper use of national emblems like the seal, the flag or the picture of Rashtrapati Bhavan. Apart from preventing insult or dishonour, the act also serves the purpose of preventing frauds being committed by impostors who claim to have governmental backing.

However, Jindal was accused of flouting something else, the Flag Code. The Flag Code was a set of executive instructions from the government restricting the flying of the flag, and specifically guiding when it could be flown. It restricted individuals from flying the flag, even though the National Emblems Act itself does not stop an individual from flying the flag. This is what Naveen Jindal challenged in Court.

Justice Wadhwa allowed the petition in favour of Naveen Jindal in 1995, mostly on the grounds that the Flag Code was not technically law and therefore could not be enforced against Jindal. Thus Jindal had won the right to fly the flag at the High Court level.

The Union of India, which is the technical name we give to the Central government, appealed the finding of the Delhi High Court. Shanti Bhushan appeared before the Supreme Court for the initial few dates. Then out of the blue, Naveen Jindal telephoned me one day and said he would like me to appear in the Supreme Court.

As is common in our court system, a number of delays followed. Justice V.N. Khare would hear the matter and then, for some reason or the other, the case would be adjourned. I joked with Justice Khare that I had walked with him as he carried the case from his old Court No. 6 to Court No. 1, the Chief's Court, when he became the Chief Justice of India. In those years from 1996 onward, the Union of India first vigorously argued against us and then tried to get the matter dismissed on the technical ground of maintainability.

When it became apparent to the government in the course of the hearings that there were some issues that they could not get around, they suggested that they would look into the issue and come back with a solution, perhaps formulate an amendment to the Flag Code. Strategically, of course, this was an attempt to find a shortcut, because the constitutional questions would have been avoided, and the final status of the flag would remain in the hands of the Union of India.

Justice Khare, although sometimes indecisive, was clear on the principle that there had been some wrong done. So, though he frequently adjourned the matter at the request of the Union of India, he did not dispose of it by the shortcut of telling the government to come back with a suitable amendment, which was a path of avoidance he could have taken.

It so happened that after almost two years of adjournments, the government ran out of ideas. On a day when I least expected it, the matter came up for hearing. That day, it was I who sought an adjournment for the first time because I realized that although I was generally prepared with the case, it raised much larger issues of constitutional law and I wanted to prepare for them.

That adjournment, which was for a few weeks, really helped to produce what I consider one of my finest written submissions. I was lucky to be able to turn the question into a larger one of constitutional importance, one that has become an important turning point in the law. For an ambitious lawyer, it is not enough to win cases – one desires to leave behind positive precedents which guide the development of the law.

The government had argued that the flying of the flag was not a fundamental right and that it did not form part of the freedom of speech and expression. This argument was based on the fact that it was mentioned in the chapter on fundamental duties. Raju Ramachandran, who was then the Additional Solicitor

General, argued that if it was a right at all, it was a right only to the extent that it permitted the citizen to carry out his duty to respect the flag.

The second main argument of the government was – how will we control the flying of the flag if it is permitted? How will we police its use by millions of people? I have always found any argument using potentially frightening consequences to be very effective on judges. A great fuss was made of it – the consequences were painted out to be disastrous.

My arguments proceeded on the following principles. First, the absurdity of the Flag Code can be shown as follows:

(1) An Indian citizen can go abroad and fly the flag of India.

(2) A foreigner abroad could fly the flag of India freely. A Pakistani in Pakistan could do so, for example.

(3) An Indian citizen in India is free to fly the flag of any other country, for example, Pakistan, in India.

(4) However, an Indian citizen in India cannot fly the flag of India.

It is blindingly clear that there is an absurdity at play here. A patriotic Indian who wants to express his or her love for their country is restricted from doing so in India, while anyone else, anywhere else, is free to do so.

My example hit home with the bench. I have found that judges are just like normal people – they respond to arguments that work on the basis of a clear example. That one can fly a Pakistani flag in India but not an Indian flag is clearly absurd. Once the idea is established in the Court's mind that there is a problem which needs fixing, the logical process of finding a way to fix it can take place.

Second, I stressed that the act of flying the flag is clearly an act of expression or speech in the wider sense of the term and is, therefore, protected by the constitutional right to the freedom of speech and expression under Article 19(1)(a). It is in fact also part of the greater right to life under Article 21, which our Courts have expanded to include the major aspects of a fulfilling and meaningful life. What more expressive way to project your patriotic feelings than flying the flag of your country respectfully.

I countered the argument of the Union that the flying of the flag is not a fundamental right but instead a fundamental duty by pointing out that one cannot separate a duty from a right. The well-established position in constitutional law is that fundamental rights and fundamental duties are like two wheels of a chariot and complement each other.

For example, if one has a right to live in a clean and healthy environment, one is also under a duty not to pollute that environment and to maintain it for others. Therefore, merely because one is under a duty to respect the flag and other symbols of the nation does not mean that there is no right to fly the flag freely. It was fundamentally an impossible argument for the government to run, but run it they did.

But what I think registered most with the bench was that our position was eminently reasonable. The difficulty with saying that the right to fly the flag is covered by the freedom of speech leads to the obvious query of whether one is free to insult the flag. In short, are we constitutionally permitted to burn the flag?

The question is not an abstract one at all. A political activist called Gregory Johnson was prosecuted by the State of Texas for burning the flag on the steps of the Dallas City Hall during a protest. In 1989 the Supreme Court of the United States held in *Texas* v. *Johnson* that however distasteful and offensive it is, a person's right to freedom of speech includes the right to burn the flag in protest. The right is constitutionally protected by the First Amendment. At one stroke, all the laws banning the desecration of the flag in the United States were rendered invalid.

As I have noted earlier, the First Amendment in the American Constitution is much wider than our corresponding rights to freedom of speech under Article 19(1)(a). The American Constitution prohibits any law from being passed which curtails free speech or expression.

Our rights under Article 19(1)(a) are explicitly subject to the exceptions set out in Article 19(2), which we call the 'reasonable restrictions' on the fundamental right. While Article 19(1)(a) says that the government will not make any law that violates the freedom of speech, Article 19(2) specifically makes exceptions for the laws that deal with national security, international relations, defamation, public order and obscenity. Within each of these categories, there is a constant tension between what is permitted and what is not – and those areas of law are evolving all the time.

Fundamentally, it was a question of culture, and that was what I put to the bench. Burning a flag was within the realm of the acceptable in America. I said that if that is the culture there, there is nothing wrong with it. What is culturally accepted ultimately becomes law in a country. India is not a country where expression of free speech can include burning the flag. I made it clear that we were not asking for that right.

So when the Court gives us a right to fly the flag, it is only a right to fly the flag *respectfully*. And that made my contention more appealing to the Court than the hard-line position which was followed in *Texas* v. *Johnson*. I could have in theory pressed for an expanded understanding of Article 19(1)(a) but I don't think it would have been right because in India we simply would not be able to culturally accept a right to trample on the flag. The Court was impressed by this affirmative concession by me, that is, a voluntary statement of the limitations of the right I was asking for.

We did a great deal of research on the history and origins of the Indian flag, on its symbolism and its role in the freedom struggle. We also researched extensively on how different countries dealt with this issue. The results are somewhat surprising. China allows for very free use of the flag, but the United Kingdom does not. Brazil allows an absolute right to fly the flag. In Brazil the flag often shows up on chappals and on all manner of garments. In India this would be culturally horrifying. Therefore, we can realistically understand what the term 'respectful' might mean in our cultural milieu.

This helped us narrow down and show the Court what we were pursuing – the right to fly the flag respectfully. Not the right to fly the flag with absolute freedom, or to have it imprinted on chappals or on bikinis. I gave these examples to the Court as clearly impermissible.

So far, so good. But now we come to the grey areas. There are clearly respectful uses and uses which are unacceptable in our country. The flag flying over an office is clearly respectful use. The flag turned into a bikini is not culturally acceptable. I take these as examples because these are binary yes or no answers and easy to decide.

The grey areas, however, are where the law is made and tested. This was what the bench put to me in the case. For example, the grey area is if you are walking in a T-shirt with a flag on it. Now, the word 'respectfully' is subjective. You can think it's respectful to wear it on your T-shirt. You may think it is not, because it is exploitation by the manufacturer/company selling the T-shirt.

I argued that the courts have to decide the question on a case-by-case basis, each on its own facts. The important point here is also what is sometimes called a hostile audience problem, which is that even if a right exists, the fact that it is hard to enforce or protect gives the state problems. Will it be socially acceptable? Perhaps not. But that is no basis or reason to deny a person the right altogether.

The Union of India fought their case using the argument of consequences. They asked, how will we control this? Once the genie is out of the bottle, how will legitimate use be differentiated from illegitimate use? One person may fly it in a respectful manner, but another may commercially exploit it, use it in a culturally derogatory manner. How do you control that?

My response was that we were not challenging the Emblems Act, and under the Emblems Act, incorrect use can be prosecuted and what constitutes incorrect use can be decided on a case-by-case basis. And for such a prosecution, the state would have to show that the user abused the right, for example, by flying the flag upside down, or torn or dirty, or mutilated with slogans. But the fact that there will be abuses is no reason to deny the right to the people. Once there is a right, it is for the state to have the machinery to prevent illegal violations of the law.

The other aspect was a more technical point on the legal standing of the Flag Code. The Flag Code was only a collection of instructions the executive gives, a bureaucratically approved document, never placed before a legislature. It was not rational or comprehensive.

In law, the question would arise as to whether such a Flag Code is actually a law in the narrow constitutional sense. We argued that it cannot be law within the technical understanding of our Constitution. Our argument was that any reasonable restriction on a fundamental right must be a positive, well-defined law either created by a legislature or a rule made under an act created by a legislature. Otherwise it cannot restrict the right. Indeed, Article 13 of the Constitution is clear that executive instructions are not 'law'.

Both the High Court and the Supreme Court agreed with us – the Flag Code would not constitute law in the legal and constitutional sense. Therefore, rights of the citizens are regulated by the Emblems Act, which is law and is a reasonable restriction on the right. The Flag Code is at the most a set of guidelines for good conduct, designed to tell an informed citizen how to act, like an FAQ. Guidelines are useful for the public, especially where the possibility of grey areas exists.

In the aftermath of these arguments and the judgement, the Flag Code was rewritten and has become more straightforward. I still think it is too long and too detailed. We are lucky that those instructions are not being used to harass people, but even so there is plenty of room for misunderstanding. In law, the position is clear, we recognize the fundamental right, and prosecution can only take place under the Emblems Act. If a citizen was expected to comply with every comma and full stop of the Flag Code, it would be very difficult. Our Flag Code therefore needs to be simplified, shortened, and made into a set of ten to twenty rules.

The truth is that actual governance under any act is done by rules and regulations. It is in the minutiae of these rules and regulations that both God and the Devil reside. An act of Parliament finally covers one-fifth of the area if it is a detailed act. Otherwise an act will cover one-hundredth of the area, and ninety-nine parts of the hundred will be covered by regulations. Those rules and regulations are made by the government, the executive, using a power specifically granted to it by the legislature – this process is called 'delegated legislation'. Further down the hierarchy are executive instructions. This is the way modern parliamentary democracies function. Some countries are born to it, and some have preferred it. I think a robust balance is still better than a complete delegation to the executive's whims and fancies and arbitrariness. We should look at examining and curing the excessively high level of delegated legislation present in our system.

It is not constitutionally healthy to have all these zombie regulations. As the British politician and judge Lord Hewart put in his classic book *The New Despotism*, which was written in the 1920s, real control is exercised by such details.

Lord Hewart was primarily concerned with the Defence of the Realm regulations. Under these regulations issued to deal with the difficulties of the First World War and then later the Second World War, millions of directions were issued, including, as an example of the absurd extent to which regulations can go, 'How to make a jelly, size, colour and malleability'. Lord Hewart's point was that this excess of petty rule-making is a kind of despotism, which can blight every aspect of our lives. We don't know whether these laws are enforceable, or whether they can be challenged in any fashion before a court. That is a thousand times truer today than it was in his era.

The Constitution of India is a great document, the statutes may be wise and carefully drafted, even our statutory notifications are issued with care, but the average citizen is overwhelmed by instructions, executive diktats and guidelines.

In the end, the Supreme Court came down thumpingly in our favour, in a beautifully written judgement by Justice V.N. Khare. It held that the right to fly the national flag is a part of the fundamental right to freedom of speech and that the right must be exercised responsibly, with respect and dignity. The Emblems and Names (Prevention of Improper Use) Act, 1950, and Prevention of Insults to National Honour Act, 1971, are reasonable restrictions on that freedom.

The Flag Code was held not to be a law in the constitutional sense, and could not restrict the flying of the flag, but could be followed as guidance. When the judgement came out, I was also pleased to find that my written submissions had been reproduced verbatim in the Supreme Court Cases – which is a rare honour.

The Union's foreboding of an unpoliceable state of affairs has manifestly not happened in the decades following the judgement. The flag has not been disrespected en masse. There are no flag burnings happening. People have used their rights respectfully, and it is a ringing endorsement of the belief we must have in the people who are the subjects of our legal system.

Flying the flag is an act of patriotism. But it is important to remember that our case was not pegged on patriotism. It is a victory for our democracy that the constitutional basis on which it was decided was not whether an act is or is not patriotic. It is based on the freedom of speech. We found a rooting in a constitutional text and unless you find a rooting in a juristic principle, you are not making good law. If the Supreme Court had said you have a right to fly the flag because it is patriotic to fly the flag, that would be uncharted and leave us without a principle to follow.

Therefore, I am happy that we pegged it and rooted it in Article 19(1)(a), which is a well-known right. Patriotism may be the underlying ethic but the judgement supports also my freedom of expression unrelated to patriotism. It is possible to use that right even in a critical sense, to use it to criticize the state of the nation. One could fly the flag at a demonstration, for example, to point out that soldiers are dying at the border for a poor policy of a government. Whether that is patriotic or not is open to question and there are people who would interpret it either way. But it is one's right – to the extent, of course, that nobody burns the flag.

One of the things I am most grateful for in the Jindal case is that the Court permitted it to be heard and decided on rights. The Union was not permitted to take it back and fix the gaps in the Flag Code, and put a soft end to the dispute. Judges who are not decisive prefer controversial disputes to be worked out broadly by consensus. That is simply a way for judges to decide not to decide. My biggest fear was the Court would back off from deciding by saying we agree there is a right, but let the government arrive at some convenient solution.

It came very close to that many times in those two to three years. These things depend largely on the personality of the judge in question. It is natural for judges to want to avoid writing a judgement if the government is telling them the decision will yield unpoliceable consequences.

But this time, Justice Khare, a little uncharacteristically, stood his ground and went on to decide the matter finally, and strongly, in our favour. Equally, even though the government had made it clear that Naveen Jindal would not be prosecuted, I am glad he decided not to withdraw the case, and allow the government to go forward with a modified Flag Code.

Naveen Jindal has invited me every year after that on 26 January, when he holds a formal flag function at his house. He always sends me a flag and also a lapel pin. I have often attended the function. As a consequence of the judgement, a flag movement started, very much encouraged by Jindal.

It started with schools educating children about the flag, then holding functions, passing out small lapel pins which children could wear. The flag movement now has become a larger movement of awareness, awareness of the unity and integrity of India through its diversity, a non-communal, secular symbol.

The flag is our most secular symbol not merely in religious terms, but also, more broadly, where secular means non-affiliated, not casteist, not sect dominated, not race dominated; it is the most secular symbol you can think of. And while this is true for every country, nowhere is it as true as in the world's most diverse country – India.

What drove Naveen Jindal to fight this long, hard,

principled fight? After all, he is an industrialist, a busy person who has plenty of important things to deal with. Why did he fight the government for years over such an abstract principle?

I think maybe it was an eccentricity. Society progresses on the backs of not only sensible people but also eccentrics and ordinary people who may have one overriding obsession. You may be a rational person, but it is the eccentric kink in you which leads to change and progress. Naveen Jindal had an unusual interest in the flag, an exceptional devotion to the cause and he fought for the principle he believed in. It is often this kind of passion, usually irrational, that wins us our rights and freedoms.

5

When Santhara Became Suicide

Nikhil Soni v. *Union of India*

The great thing about the practice of the law is how many people it can touch. Sometimes it can be very dry and abstract, a tender for coal supply, a suit for damages, a challenge to a tax demand. Sometimes it can literally mean determining the philosophical difference between life and death.

In 2015 the Rajasthan High Court bench at Jaipur passed a shocking order in a case called *Nikhil Soni v. Union of India.* The effect of the order was that the ancient practice of the Jain community called santhara became illegal overnight.

I came to be involved at the Supreme Court level when the Jain community came to me to appeal against the order. I was shocked by the verdict and I took up the cudgels immediately, and we succeeded in having the judgement stayed. The case remains one of the more interesting matters I have worked on, although the order I obtained is laughably plain and only three sentences long. It reads as follows:

> Permission to file special leave petition(s) is granted.
> Leave granted.
> During the pendency of the appeal(s), there shall be interim stay of the impugned judgement and order passed by the High Court of Judicature for Rajasthan at Jaipur Bench in D.B. Civil Writ Petition No. 7414 of 2006.

To a non-lawyer, this gnomic utterance may not say much. What it means is that while the question is still to be finally decided at some distant point in the future, at this point the Jain community is free to continue with one of its venerable practices. As with many cases, it is often what lies behind the order and what happened before the order was passed that is of the greatest importance.

What is santhara, and why did the Rajasthan High Court see fit to declare it illegal? Santhara or sallekhana is the ancient Jain practice of a person calmly and happily accepting death at the end of a long and fully lived life. The ritual is undergone when a person has reached extreme old age or has terminal illness or has been victim to a natural calamity – situations where the end is inevitable.

At that point, that person takes a vow of santhara and ceases to accept food or water and waits for the end of life. The vow is taken alongside the family who remain with the individual, with the full knowledge of the community, and is viewed as an act of acceptance and courage. The person who has taken santhara prepares his or her mind and body for the most natural of all things, the end of life.

The High Court verdict came out of a PIL which was filed by a man called Nikhil Soni, who was not a Jain and did not have a great understanding of the practice. He asked the Court why it was permitted for Jains to 'take their life'? Surely, such an action was equivalent to suicide, which is not permitted by the laws of India.

The law, of course, cannot punish suicide itself, for very obvious reasons. But it can and does punish the attempt to commit suicide, and certainly abetment to suicide, which can sometimes be murder by disguised means.

The petitioner in Rajasthan wanted the Court to declare that santhara or Sallekhana were also acts of suicide and, therefore, should be illegal. If so, anyone who assisted a person in taking a vow of santhara would have committed a crime under Section 306 of the Indian Penal Code (IPC). And the person who had taken the vow should be prosecuted under Section 309 of the IPC.

To help us understand what their case was, let us look at Section 306 and Section 309 of the IPC:

306. Abetment of suicide. If any person commits suicide, whoever abets the commission of such suicide, shall be punished with imprisonment of either description for a term which may extend to ten years, and shall also be liable to fine.

309. Attempt to commit suicide. Whoever attempts to commit suicide and does any act towards the commission of such offence, shall be punished with simple imprisonment for a term which may extend to one year or with fine, or with both.

This argument can be attractive, at the most superficial level, in the absence of the knowledge of what the law protects and what it does not, and in the ignorance of the historical and philosophical dimensions of the practice of santhara.

I am a Jain and I have always believed that the essence of Jainism lies not in its form, not in its rituals, not even so much in its history and mythology, but in its philosophy, which is among the world's deepest, and most complex.

Jainism is extraordinary because of its remarkable rationality, its insistence on logic and its abstraction of thought. It is not for nothing that Jainism is the only religion, of the known major religions, which is sometimes considered *too* rational, *too* severe.

The religion embraces many difficult concepts – for example, it has no big bang theory, no story of creation, no creationist moment, it says instead '*anaadhi anantam chha*' which means 'it is there, it is always to be there'. To most of us, this explanation is harder to accept than any story, no matter how fanciful, which can explain how from nothing comes everything. It brings comfort to have a story to hang on to.

There is no god to appeal to – Jainism is atheistic by nature. Jainism espoused ideas like the relativity of time and space, millennia before Einstein got there through scientific means. In Jainism these principles of relative relations are referred to as *sapekshwaad* or *syad veda*.

The biggest contribution of Jainism to Indian history is the idea of ahimsa – non-violence. The ahimsa movement, which won us freedom from the British, was as powerful as an atom bomb. Mahatma Gandhi acknowledged many times his debt to Jainism, which was taught to him by Acharya Rajbhadra. Of course, it was Gandhi's genius which converted a general principle into a political weapon by coupling it with the European school of civil disobedience.

The many conversations around environmental sustainability we are having today have strong parallels in Jainism, where there is a deep respect for life of all forms, from the lowest to the highest. Almost all the arguments we see today in that field – intergenerational equity, environmental sustainability, the polluter pays principle, maintaining ecosystem balances – have direct parallels in Jain philosophy and writings as well. From algae to humans, all life is sacred in Jainism.

In his book *Sanskriti Ke Char Adhyay,* the great Hindi poet and scholar Ramdhari Singh Dinkar observed that the word traditionally used in India for a holy man is *rishi* and it is only over time that the word *muni* came into existence.

Rishi and muni have totally different origins. The word rishi has Vedic roots and during that period a rishi was a *bhogi*, a powerful warrior, who would eat meat, including beef, live a full life, have many wives, and also be a great sage who was considered learned in the Vedas.

The muni, however, is one who abstains, who gives up, who turns away from the worldly. That word and idea come from Jainism. The very concept of *tyaag*, of sacrifice, is a Jain contribution to Indian thinking. The rishi, unlike the muni, never practised abstinence, from eating, or sex, or life.

From these Jain ideas of abstinence and sacrifice comes the entire *sanskriti* of vows, celibacy, denial, *upwaas*, *ekashna*, etc., which are now part of the fabric of most of the faiths of the subcontinent. Today when we say rishi-muni, we erase the distinction between, and origins of, these two words.

Jainism is closely linked with Buddhism in the public mind, as a later reformist faith, but it is much older and is in fact older even than Hinduism. No less a thinker than S. Radhakrishnan found that Jainism is much older, in its epistemology, and a separate but equally ancient religion and culture as Vedic Hinduism. Mahavira, if you recall, preceded the Buddha in the sixth century BCE, but he was also the twenty-fourth Tirthankara – and the twenty-three before him were also Jains.

Jainism has existed in one form or the other since at least 3000 BC. For centuries, Jainism has been viewed as a reformist strain of Hinduism, but it is an independent religion that actually has nothing to do with Hinduism. It never broke away from Hinduism but ran parallel to it. India was once full of Jain empires. Those parts we now call Karnataka, Rajasthan, Gujarat and Bihar were majority Jain during the Iron Age. All the great emperors of ancient India were Jains or embraced Jainism, except Ashoka, who became Buddhist. Ashoka's father and grandfather were Jains, a fact that is frequently left out of mainstream history.

Over the millennia, Jainism has become ritualistic in practice. In Mahavira's time there were no Digambars and Shwetambars, and now besides Digambars and Shwetambars there are dozens of subsects. Today, Jains differentiate themselves over the purely ritualistic parts of the religion.

In the twenty-first century, Jainism and the

understanding of Jainism are dwindling – and much of what we see is just the severity of the restrictions orthodox Jains put themselves under. From being a thriving community, Jainism is now India's smallest minority, after Zoroastrianism.

Now there are very few of us, and it is in part because of the severity of the faith. The great teacher Acharya Mahapragya, who died a few years ago, never travelled as widely as his less orthodox peers because he would not go anywhere except by walking barefoot, a mandatory practise for renowned Jain sages.

While some preachers and holy men from other faiths will now fly and preach around the world, he would not even take a bullock cart. I tried once to explain to him that he could do so much good if he just drove and covered a few hundred kilometres a month. But his principles, the strength of his will and the severe principles of Jainism would not let him.

The wisdom of these teachers is, therefore, contained. They have tremendous philosophies, but their reach is limited, and that is one reason why Jainism has dwindled and there is a great deal of ignorance regarding the religion and its philosophy.

Jains were not even considered a minority in India

since they were regarded as a sect of Hindus until a recent Supreme Court judgement. This despite the fact that the faiths are different, the texts are different, and norms and practices are completely different.

It is in this context that we come back to the judgement of the Rajasthan High Court in Nikhil Soni's case. It was born of ignorance. The petitioner was a stranger who had no direct interest in the matter at all. He was not a Jain or in any way related to the community. He was merely a person who had seen some newspaper reports of persons taking a vow of santhara.

The respondents, who would have been the Jain organizations, were not at first before the Court. The matter was filed by the petitioner against the government, the Union of India. The Jain organizations had to come and plead themselves, by explaining to the Court that they were necessary and proper parties to the litigation, that without hearing them the Court could not appreciate the matter. The entire matter proceeded on an examination of cases on suicide – on interpretations of the two judgements of *Gian Kaur* and *Aruna Shanbaug*.

In the *Gian Kaur* case, the question asked in Court was whether Section 306 and Section 309 were constitutionally valid. Article 21 in our Constitution says everyone has a right to life. The petitioner argued that meant everyone has a right to die as well, which would make both Sections 306 and 309 invalid.

The Court answered that it did not – and there was no basis for striking down the sections as unconstitutional. In the case of Section 309, this was interesting because the Court had earlier in the *P. Rathinam* case in 1994 held that there was a right to die implicit in the right to life, and, therefore, an attempt at suicide could not be punished. *Gian Kaur* was essentially a conservative reversal of that 1994 judgement.

Aruna Shanbaug was a very sad case which fortunately did result in some advance in the law. Aruna Shanbaug was a nurse at a hospital in Bombay, where one night in 1973 she was brutally assaulted and raped, and entered into a coma where she remained until her death in 2015.

In 2010 an activist approached the Supreme Court urging that in cases such as that of Aruna Shanbaug, a person in a persistent vegetative state may be granted a right to passive euthanasia as keeping them nominally alive is merely keeping them in suffering. The Supreme Court held in 2011 that in a narrow set of cases, passive euthanasia would be permissible, and laid down conditions to prevent abuse, such as written consent of the family, consent from a medical board, etc.

Nikhil Soni v. *Union of India* had been moving along slowly in the Rajasthan High Court as our cases tend to do when suddenly the bench decided it had heard enough and passed the order. The order is devoid of any kind of legal reasoning.

It reflects the standard vice of some Indian court orders – reproduce submissions, note down the arguments made, and then in the last one or two pages proceed on to what it thinks is the point. There is no examination of the arguments, weighing of pros and cons, or testing the arguments against the law laid down earlier.

The High Court only looked narrowly at the *Gian Kaur* and *Aruna Shanbaug* judgements – arguing that the *Gian Kaur* judgement had shown clearly that suicide was not a natural right in our Constitution, and the only exceptions to be made were in cases such as *Aruna Shanbaug*. But I believe they got even their reading of *Gian Kaur* and *Aruna Shanbaug* wrong. When evaluating a question of constitutional importance, they did not adequately consider the Constitution and case law on the right to religious freedom.

Our Constitution protects as a fundamental right the freedom of conscience, and as part of that, the freedom to profess, practise and propagate religion without interference from the state. These words are of the widest amplitude – not only is there the freedom to hold and state a belief, but also to outwardly exhibit and practise it.

Since there is no one way to define a religion, ethical rules, codes, rituals and observances, ceremonies, modes of worship, matters of food and dress, all may, in the context, form an integral and essential part of the religion. As an example of what the courts treat as a non-essential part of religion are matters of an economic, commercial or political nature.

But the decision on what is and what is not essential must be seen within the specific context of that doctrine or religion itself. The Courts in India have over the last seventy years tested the concept of an essential religious practice extensively, and yet it arises again and again, each time contentious and controversial. This is interesting, especially today.

An essential religious practice cannot, of course, be something which hurts other people or causes a breakdown of law and order or which is morally offensive. You cannot, for example, defend an adherent for killing an unbeliever as an essential religious practice. Nor can you defend cannibalism. But within these very wide bounds, our Constitution does guarantee freedom to practise one's faith.

For example, in one case where the right to slaughter cows for Eid came into conflict with a law against cow slaughter, the Court went into the question of the essentiality of that narrow practice. It found that while the sacrifice of an animal was absolutely an essential religious practice, it was not essential that it must be a cow, and a sheep or goat was equally acceptable. Therefore, the ban on cow slaughter was allowed to stand, as it did not necessarily offend the essential religious practice of a community.

This may seem unusual to an outsider. So I can slaughter any other animal for the purpose of sacrifice but not a cow? And if so, who are you to tell me that, not being a religious authority I believe in? When the Court enters questions of religion, sometimes there are results which do not appear rational, or which seem rational to the outsider but cause anger in that particular religious community. It is one of the inevitable tensions in our constitutional structure.

A similar controversial case dealing with the concept of essential religious practices was the Sabarimala case, discussed earlier. The same set of principles contained in Articles 25 and 26 of the Constitution would be applicable here.

There is a problem with the way our courts process such matters as PILs. Now, if I am a person with some rights which are critical for me, I am forced to defend them as a respondent. The petitioner is a person with no right and no case really. He has no skin in the game. In a PIL, it is not the victim before the court, nor the victim's family, but some interested outsider who feels that the common good will be served with such a petition.

Who with actual knowledge of the alleged suicides was standing before the Court? No one. So as a result, you have an academic question, which is always a dangerous thing to lay before judges. If you look at the cases of santhara laid before the Court, one person was ninety-three, another was ninety-four and yet another was ninety-seven.

At those ages, the unusual occurrence is not death, but continued life. In none of these instances was there an investigation or an enquiry or a whisper or suspicion around the deaths, only the celebration of a long and happy life which had come to a natural end.

Forty-one of the forty-six pages of the High Court judgement are a mechanical repetition of rival contentions – who said what in Court. The last four pages perfunctorily reach a conclusion, without referring to the history or detailed material on the origins and history of the custom that had been laid before the Court.

The organizations representing the Jain communities came to me because of the prominence of our family in the Jain community. My father was a leader of the Jain community in his time. I took on the matter pro bono, as did a number of other well-known lawyers of the Supreme Court. Lawyers of different subsects of Jainism, between whom there would have been many differences on any ordinary matter, all united behind this common cause.

Upon looking into the matter, I realized I would need a great deal of assistance and research. I got hold of books which are out of print, I talked to people and had long conferences that went on late into the night. All of which ultimately resulted in that three-sentence order we started this chapter with.

The first step was to be able to prove essentiality – that is, the practice in question was an integral part of the religion – as in any case under Article 25. This is the first step, without which we are out of court on the issue of religious freedom. We worked at building a great deal of material on the history of the practice to show that there was overwhelming evidence historically, scripturally and archaeologically that santhara is an essential part of Jainism.

Just to give you a taste of the extent of the evidence on the issue:

(1) There are hundreds of shlokas in the sacred texts of the Jains, including the *Ratnakarandaka Shravakchara*, *Tattvartha Sutra*, *Uttaradhyayana Sutra* and *Sachitra Acharang Sutra*. These texts are all more than 1500 years old.

(2) Rock inscriptions from Koppal district near Mysore from the third century BC show hundreds of commoners, kings and queens all being commemorated for renouncing the world and taking a vow of santhara.

(3) Even Chandragupta Maurya, who is well known to all students of Indian history, took santhara at the end of his life.

A cursory review of the available historical and theological literature on the topic would be sufficient to convince a reasonable person of the essential nature of the practice and its historicity. It is shocking that the High Court did not see any of this material before passing the order in *Nikhil Soni*.

The moment something is found to be an essential religious practice, the burden to protect it becomes very strong. To then injunct it in law, you have to argue an issue of public order, health or morality, which in the constitutional context are very high bars to reach. None of those arguments were raised, and none are really applicable.

In any case, and this is the very basic second argument, santhara is fundamentally different from suicide, which is what ignorant people have equated it with. Jainism abhors himsa or violence, and suicide is a violent taking of one's life. Santhara is non-violent in its very principle. There is no violent act, merely an acceptance of the inevitable.

There are strict scriptural preconditions to santhara, as I have noted earlier. Once these are met a Jain will then embark on the ultimate renunciation. After seeking forgiveness from those he feels he has offended or hurt, he makes every attempt to divorce himself from any attachment to life. Santhara is typically done with the whole family sitting around. One takes a vow, one meditates and stops eating or drinking. That is the difference between santhara and suicide. Suicide in Jain philosophy is in fact rejected as being a childish or foolish action.

The Jaipur High Court had been led astray by the petitioner who had ignorantly equated santhara with sati. No two things could be further apart! Sati is illegal by virtue of an act of Parliament – santhara only by virtue of this judgement on an erroneous interpretation. Sati – even when it is not compelled – is an act of suicide. Sati is usually compelled when it happens, and santhara is never compelled – a quick look at the High Court petitioner's own examples with which he approached the Court would show people having taken santhara at the ages of ninety-three, ninety-four and ninety-seven. Sati, for example, could never meet the test of being an essential religious practice, and could not be defended even if it were.

These were the arguments we put forth in our petition to the Supreme Court, and that is the basis for the order which was passed by the Court. There will never be a large number of people taking a vow of santhara – it is a tremendously difficult thing to do, but the case was about so much more.

To me the issue was about curtailing an essential religious practice, and on behalf of someone who had no relationship with it. Can outsiders to religious communities force their values on the realm of private faith?

On the larger philosophical question of a right to die or a right to commit suicide – it is a complicated question, philosophically and legally. Societies and religions all over the world have different norms and standards for right behaviour. For example, while in some societies cannibalism is permissible, in most societies it isn't. Murder, however, is seen as wrong across all cultures. So also suicide across most cultures is considered impermissible.

What cultures do disagree on is whether the attempt to commit suicide ought to be criminalized. Many countries which consider the attempt to commit suicide impermissible or immoral or wrong do not criminalize it. India criminalizes it.

The debate was not about suicide being wrong, the debate was about criminalizing it. In other words, even if it is wrong, you should not criminalize it because you end up only punishing the attempt. You can't punish the crime. However, the more complicated question is – is suicide wrong at all?

I would lean towards the middle ground. Suicide should be an illegal act but not necessarily one which attracts a criminal punishment, because that does not serve a positive end. Perhaps medical or psychiatric intervention is the best antidote to a case of attempted suicide.

Classically, we look to the harm principle when we study laws. The harm principle was J.S. Mill's enlightenment era test for interference with personal liberty. In short, it reasons that if I am not harming anybody with my actions, I should be free to pursue them.

When my freedom encroaches on somebody else's right, it may be curtailed, but to do so otherwise is tyranny. Many of our laws are indefensible when placed against this principle; the fact is we do have paternalistic laws. All modern societies do, India is far from alone. In our societies, we are stopped from harming ourselves with drugs, for example, and we are warned off alcohol and cigarette smoking.

In an abstract sense there may be a right to commit suicide – but those abstractions are part of no state's laws. Determining where a state can interfere paternalistically is an ongoing enterprise – for example, in recent times, we have evicted the state from the bedroom with judgements reading down unnatural sex and adultery. These are all chapters in the story of a society determining the boundaries its citizens may live within.

6

Shareholder Democracy and Its Discontents

Cyrus Mistry v. *Tata Sons*

We celebrate the great constitutional cases – the important questions of rights of citizens and how far the law can go, but most of our work deals with commercial matters. After all, most disagreements between people are about very predictable things – who owns what part of a building or a piece of land, or who was owed money or goods in a business deal, or what somebody's shares in a company entitle them to.

Because a huge amount of money usually rides upon them, the biggest of these corporate battles often involve the best legal talent. Crack teams of lawyers from the big law firms work night and day and brief top counsel. As a result, the arguments are often very creative.

My first brush with such battles took place in the early 1990s, when the Shaw Wallace brothers, Manu and Kishore Chhabria, were fighting each other in courts across India. I used to lead the arguments even then, except in the Supreme Court, where I used to appear with Anil Divan.

As our economy opened up during liberalization, so did cases of commercial litigation. In terms of size of the businesses and stakes involved, those cases of the early 1990s look very small compared to the battles today. Of these, in recent years, nothing has attracted more eyeballs than the war between Tata and Cyrus Mistry.

The Tata group is probably the most pre-eminent of all Indian business houses, not only in size and breadth, but also in terms of their heritage and what they have meant to the country over the last 150 years. When Jamsetji Tata founded Tata Sons in 1868, he brought into existence the first Indian industrial business, laid down the foundation of technical education, created the steel and power industries and made it possible for the modern nation of India to start taking its infant steps.

Since then, the history of Tatas and the history of India have been inseparable. It was Tata Airlines which became Air India and Indian Airlines. The Tata group started with oil mills, spread into the key industries of steel and power and from there into every part of daily life in India, and today occupies a major, if not always dominant, place in industries across India, from tea and hotels to cars and telecom.

Tata Sons became the controlling parent of the Tata group of companies, the holding company, and remains the jewel in the Tata crown. Throughout the 150-year heritage of the company, only six people have been the chairmen of Tata Sons, which sits at the top of the whole empire of the Tata group.

From Jamsetji Tata, who was chairman for thirty-six years, the seat came to Sir Dorab Tata, who was chair for twenty-eight years, and who started the trusts which have given so much philanthropically. Nowroji Saklatwala was chairman for a relatively brief six years in the 1930s, and then J.R.D. Tata took over in 1938.

From 1938 to 1991 J.R.D. Tata was not only the chairman of the company, but also a pillar of Indian business and industry. It was under his guidance that civil aviation, for one, emerged in India. From 1991 to 2012 his nephew Ratan Tata guided the company into the bold new world of the global markets as the Indian giant embarked on some of the most daring adventures yet undertaken by an Indian business. It was under his stewardship that Tata bought global businesses like Corus Steel and Jaguar Land Rover. In one of my meetings with Ratan, I told him that many Indians, including myself, were proud of this reverse imperialism of the British!

But in 2012 even Ratan Tata had to retire, and there was no obvious heir to the seat of chairman. A search commenced for a young, dynamic new leader who could guide the company in a millennial world. That man, installed with great pomp and ceremony, was Cyrus Mistry.

Cyrus Mistry had been a director at various Tata companies since 2006 and was the heir of the Shapoorji Pallonji construction business. His appointment was celebrated as the beginning of a brave new era. It was only the second time in Tata history that someone without the 'Tata' name would be the chairman. To outsiders, it might seem like a vote in favour of professional, non-family, management.

The truth is more complex. The families had long been connected, both by marriage and by shareholding. Shapoorji Pallonji held a major stake in Tata Sons, approximately 18.4 per cent of the equity shares of the company. The great majority of the shares of Tata Sons are held by a handful of trusts – the biggest among which are the Sir Dorabji Tata Trust and the Sir Ratan Tata Trust.

The idea behind having a set of trusts holding ultimate control of the shares was to lend an intergenerational stability to the business and to ensure the guiding hand of the elder members of the Tata family. So when Cyrus Mistry came into the company, he was inevitably going to be guided by the trusts, and the face of those trusts was naturally Ratan Tata.

There were tensions, and they grew and rankled. Cyrus Mistry was concerned by some of the business problems he had inherited. For example, the Corus acquisition had turned troublesome, and the Nano car, which had been one of Ratan Tata's pet projects, had not been as popular as expected in the market. Ratan Tata and some other board members had been disappointed with Cyrus's decision-making and concerned that they were not always informed about issues which were to be discussed at board meetings, even though they represented the majority of shareholders.

At 2 p.m. on 24 October 2016 a board meeting was to take place at Tata Sons, chaired by Cyrus Mistry. Nothing especially unusual was slated to happen at the meeting, and the agenda did not contain any surprises – primarily investments in AirAsia.

Cyrus Mistry took the chair and was confronted by

the directors representing the Tata Trusts and told that since the relationship between the board and himself had not been working, he was being asked to step down as chairman and managing director.

Cyrus Mistry immediately asked why this was not on the agenda. He was informed that it was not legally necessary and that the company had sought legal opinions to back that up. Then, as he did not of his own accord step down, a resolution was moved to remove him as chairman. Two directors abstained, and the rest voted for his exit. No one voted for his continuance.

It was all over in an hour. Cyrus Mistry had been removed from one of the most coveted managerial spots in the world. He would continue as a director, which he had been since the year 2006, but he was no longer the head of Tata Sons. He was to clear out his office and leave Bombay House. His own council of employees who were outsiders were sacked with immediate effect as well. In the meantime, Ratan Tata was appointed interim chairman, and the company began to look for a permanent replacement. By the end of the day, the dramatic events were all over the press. Even the share markets were stunned.

Cyrus Mistry went immediately to court. The court

he chose to approach was the National Company Law Tribunal (NCLT) in a kind of case called an 'oppression and mismanagement' case. This is unusual because it is not an action you pursue in order to enforce, for example, an employment agreement or to seek damages. It is a case you file supposedly to protect your rights as a shareholder who meets a certain minimum criterion of shareholding. The NCLTs are specialized company law courts which handle cases of corporate insolvency and shareholder disputes. These cases do not go before the regular courts; by law they must go to the NCLT.

A company is a democracy in a sense – it will do the will of the majority of shareholders. But where a minority of shareholders is obviously squeezed out, or deprived of the value of their shareholding, against the law, and against the interest of the company, they can seek relief in a petition for oppression and mismanagement.

But Cyrus Mistry himself did not hold significant shares. Those shares were held by the Shapoorji Pallonji companies. They filed a petition against Tata Sons, and Cyrus Mistry was a respondent party supporting them. Shapoorji Pallonji were claiming that their voice on the board of Tata Sons was being drowned out.

At this point, Ratan Tata called me to take on this fight, and warned me that it would be a big one. I had not met him earlier and was pleased to find him a dignified, balanced, solid and sober person, not flashy or ostentatious in the least.

I knew that this case would be a long-drawn one. It had started with a rush of anger on both sides. In most cases like this where the litigants are proud, the anger remains inflamed for some time, then cooler heads win and a settlement is reached. But I didn't expect this to happen here as the issues were more deep-rooted and both sides had enormous resources.

This being a very prestigious, major battle, I had a team of about twelve people with me, including four or five senior advocates whom I led. With me were Ravi Kadam from Bombay, Mohan Parasaran of Delhi (former Solicitor General of India), S.N. Mukherjee of Calcutta, Zal Andhyarujina and many others. The other side was led by C. Aryama Sundaram but they had a smaller team overall. Janak Dwarkadas was personally appearing for Cyrus Mistry.

At the first stage, the fight was about two things: interim measures and maintainability. From December 2016 to January 2017 every attempt was made by the petitioners to get some kind of interim order. It wasn't even a very important thing they were seeking, but they wanted a victory, any victory. They had to save face somehow after the ouster.

They were coming from a position where their man had been sacked, and so they felt they had lost something and needed to have a win. So they pleaded that there were various things which required interim protection. An interim or interlocutory order is not a final decision on anything, but merely an arrangement directed by the court to prevent anything from going awry while the case is being heard.

Now I think interim protections are sometimes really ego trips, and have very little practical use. If a property is in danger of being destroyed, an interim protection might save it, and that is a valid case. But where a person has been removed from a management position, then in the course of hearing whether he should or should not have been, a court is very unlikely to reverse the removal. But because he was on a losing wicket, Cyrus Mistry wanted to score a symbolic victory by having some kind of an order in his favour.

Unfortunately, in high-profile cases, the press impressions and perceptions of the public are more important than the actual thing. So if you sneezed, it would be reported. There was a lot of misreporting and it was alleged by our side that the other side tended to place stories in the media which were not exactly what transpired in Court.

I am proud to say I prevented any interim orders from being passed. On each of those attempts an appeal was also put forth to the National Company Law Appellate Tribunal (NCLAT) in Delhi but there too requests by Mistry were turned down. Mistry's side thus did not get the satisfaction of an interim order, even a symbolic one.

Maintainability – whether a case meets the basic requirements to be filed and heard – is a battle where the petitioners did succeed though later at the appellate stage of the NCLAT after having lost even maintainability at the primary level of the NCLT. Our objection was on the technical ground that in order to maintain a petition before the NCLT, a shareholder or group of shareholders must either be more than a hundred individuals or one-tenth of all individuals, or must hold at least 10 per cent of the issued share capital of the company.

A company is a democracy, after all, and while each shareholder has rights, a tiny group cannot be permitted to defeat the rights of the vast majority. That is why the law contains this qualificatory hurdle – if you have more than 10 per cent, you can come to the NCLT seeking protection. Even taken together, the Shapoorji Pallonji companies only held 2.17 per cent of the share capital of Tata Sons.

But wait, you may ask, didn't I tell you earlier that they held 18.4 per cent of the equity of Tata Sons, and were the third biggest shareholders after the two Tata Trusts? That is true, but there are two kinds of share capital, equity and preference. Equity is what the Shapoorji Pallonji companies held 18.4 per cent of, and that entitled them to voting rights; equity is closest to the conception of 'ownership' of a company. Preference shares are more like a debt or borrowing – they do not usually carry voting rights, and therefore they can be issued to raise money more freely, because the promoters of companies do not necessarily lose control while raising money.

In Tata Sons, the total equity share capital amounted to Rs 40 crore and the total preference share capital stood at Rs 294 crore. Taken together, the 18.4 per cent of the equity shares that Cyrus Mistry's companies held represented what was actually only 2.17 per cent of the total issued shares. Therefore, as they were less than 10 per cent of the issued share capital, they could not have maintained the petition they had filed.

However, one further route was open to them, which was to seek special dispensation to maintain the petition because of unusual circumstances, a waiver of the rule. This they succeeded in obtaining, not at first from the NCLT in Bombay, where they lost on maintainability as well as on injunction, but from the NCLAT in appeal. The main reason the NCLAT allowed them the wavier was that as the shareholding stood, only the Tata Trusts could ever meet the threshold 10 per cent condition, and to do so, even they would have to band together.

If the provision was to provide minority protection in such circumstances, a waiver would have to be granted. The high proportion of the relative value of the minority shareholding in the company, that is, about one lakh crore out of a value of six lakh crore, was also key in the NCLAT granting a waiver.

All of that, hundreds and hundreds of man-hours, before judges and in preparation, was only a skirmish. The main battle lay ahead.

The NCLT Bombay bench itself had a problem with setting a schedule for the hearings, because there were so many busy lawyers involved, and a lot of adjustments were made. It also involved persons like me and many others assisting me to displace ourselves from Delhi to go to Bombay. The matter was heard in three-day blocks, over months, in aggregate a few weeks' worth of dates, but set apart to allow us all to function.

I had to go through a lot of painful scheduling, but it was also oddly relaxing to be away from Delhi, focusing on one case during those weeks. After a while you know the case inside out (so the preparation does not have to be as lengthy each time, although we had put in long hours of preparation initially) and you can relax. It is also always a pleasure working in Bombay because the bar there is a little more professional and a little less aggressive than it is in Delhi – perhaps something that can be said about the cities more generally as well.

Cyrus Mistry and his companies had pegged their case on the argument that the Tata Trusts did not permit him to function with a free hand and that Ratan Tata had never actually let him have real management. The Articles of Association – documents which lay down the rules of how the company is run – of the Trust made it impossible for anyone to function with true independence. Therefore, he was also seeking the striking down of those articles.

In his arguments he described the existing structure as one with 'shadow directors' and 'super boards'. These 'super boards' were allegedly controlled by Ratan Tata and the Tata Trusts' trustee Noshir Soonawala, with the independent directors on the boards not allowed to function independently.

To back up his arguments he took to a review of the decisions in which he felt he had been interfered with by the board, from having to invest in AirAsia in 2013 where he claimed frauds had taken place, being forced to set up Vistara Airlines with Singapore Airlines as a partner which he felt was financially unwise.

He claimed that Tata Teleservices was prejudicially affected by Ratan Tata's relationship with C. Sivasankaran of Sterling, particularly in losses incurred while dealing with NTT DoCoMo, the Japanese telecom major. He claimed that his planned issue of shares of Tata Motors was stymied, sales of businesses were delayed and interfered with. And that price-sensitive information was constantly being sought from the board.

Cyrus Mistry also claimed to be aggrieved by what he had walked into. According to him, some of the divisions were performing very poorly and it had fallen to him to turn them around. He felt that bad business decisions were being clung to for emotional reasons such as the continuation of the Tata Nano, which had been a dream of Ratan Tata's. He described these as 'legacy hotspots' or 'white elephants'. His strategy was to get out of failing businesses and write off losses instead of throwing good money after bad.

Mistry cited the example of Tata's acquisition of Corus Steel saying that it had left the company with underperforming European assets which had been bought at a high cost, and that it was loaded with debt and pension liabilities. He also wanted to write off assets and restructure the balance sheets of Indian Hotels Company – in some of these, the assets he wanted to write off were prestige projects such as the Pierre hotel in New York. He felt, however, that the older heads at the Trusts were more concerned with the image of these assets than in their viability financially.

He also pointed to the results of poor or compromised decision-making, an alleged fraud at AirAsia worth Rs 22 crore and an unconscionable decision by Tata Teleservices not to litigate against C. Sivasankaran and Sterling.

From our side, the argument was much more simple and rooted in law instead of highly disputed facts.

Each of the issues he had raised had factual points and counterpoints. There was data to show the wisdom of every decision or the lack of it. All of these were also argued, but that is not what turned the case in our favour.

Cyrus Mistry was employed pursuant to a contract like any other employee of Tata Sons and was answerable to the board and ultimately to the shareholders represented on the board. The moment he lost their confidence, for better or worse, he had to go. The public was largely unaware that Mistry was actually on a five-year contract. He was not unceremoniously thrown out. He was firmly asked to leave. He did not leave and, therefore, he was voted out as chairman. He was still kept on as a director.

His shock at the historical state of various businesses or the decisions made could be understandable if he were truly an outsider, brought in and handed an unsteerable ship. But he had been on the board from 2006, and in individual companies even earlier. Each of the legacy hotspots, each of the white elephants he pointed to, was one that he had been in a position to caution about at the time they were entered into.

But he did not do so for more than a decade, and in fact in all of those decisions, he voted in favour of them. For him to now turn around and say he was saddled with them was unfair, highly opportunistic and highly selective. Documents showed that his complaints had arisen in the few months leading up to the crisis when his personal equations with Ratan Tata and Noshir Soonawaala had gone south.

His arguments against the articles themselves being unfair were far-fetched, I argued. Those articles had been there long before he was selected, and the shareholding of the companies had been in place since the 1960s. The structure with the Tata Trusts holding a controlling stake in the Tata Sons company had existed for almost a hundred years. In fact, those articles were amended and the amendments had been endorsed by him from time to time. Suddenly, when he fell afoul of them, the articles seemed problematic to him.

The argument of a super board being in place is just a fancy way of saying that an affirmative vote was required on certain major decisions. I argued that you could open the books of any company of any reasonable size and would find similar affirmative provisions – they would always exist to protect key shareholders. In fact, historically, those powers have never been exercised at Tata Sons, who believed that they have never been needed to be used.

But Cyrus Mistry, I argued, had failed in his duties to the board. He had failed to provide the Trusts and the members of the board with information on decisions in advance, and had failed to allow them to make informed decisions consistently. In doing so, he had acted as if he himself were the whole of the board, and this was why he had fallen out of favour with the shareholders.

It was also alleged that Cyrus Mistry had sent cartons of documents to the Income Tax Department after his dismissal as chairman, but while he was still a director. This had resulted in notices being issued to individuals as well as the company. According to our side, he was acting as a Trojan horse inside the company, completely against its interests.

Let us assume that the board's decision was wrong and prejudiced. Let us assume that Cyrus Mistry was the greatest possible manager and it was a horrible mistake to sack him. The point is that you cannot, and equally a judge cannot, judge corporate decision-making by these standards.

The company is legally a person, and the board is its mind. That board is composed of directors who in turn are nominated by the shareholders. Every employee is the servant of the company. One cannot have an unwilling master with an undesirable servant foisted upon him. One cannot compel a relationship which requires trust and confidence every day, that too by court injunction.

It is as simple as saying that your servant may be right, but you cannot work with him. You cannot be in the same house if you have lost confidence. Even Steve Jobs, who founded Apple, was removed from Apple by its board – that is how corporate democracy works.

That is what happened, we reminded the Court. He was voted out by six out of nine board members. One was himself, who did not vote, and two abstained. He did not get a single vote in his favour and none against the motion to remove him – the mind of the company had been made up.

Mistry had been unable to carry the board along with him. If six out of nine voted against you, and the other two merely abstained, there is only one conclusion – that you failed to carry them with you.

All the directors of Tata Sons are in fact of rare pedigree. They include a former defence secretary, a top financial wizard, a former ambassador to the United States and a current dean of the Harvard Business

School. They are all well known and respected. Some of them are designated as independent directors, as per the Companies Act, and are beholden to none of the shareholders.

Now to imagine that all were collectively conspiring against Mr Mistry and then acted against him out of bias is unlikely. When Cyrus Mistry complains about shadow directors and says that they are all biased in favour of, or voting on the directions of, Ratan Tata, he, according to us, ignores that this too is a feature of corporate democracy. That if an otherwise independent director can be persuaded to vote a certain way on the basis of the business advice or acumen of one person, that is a perfectly legitimate way to vote.

Tata Sons tried to behave decently with Cyrus Mistry. He was still kept on as director for more than four months. He was given an option to leave from the other Tata operating companies as well. He did neither. He could have said, 'I do not agree with your actions, but I am exiting from this and the other companies.' I do not blame him for this obstinacy, I blame his advisers.

The Tata operating companies are not minor subsidiaries of Tata Sons. Tata Motors, Tata Steel and Tata Consultancy Services are giants by any global standards. He tried to hold on to the chairs of those companies and did not leave till he was voted out, and so he brought bad blood upon himself.

He then started filing a number of defamation suits and defamation complaints, which caused the fight to get even more personal. Those matters are sub judice and so it would not be advisable to discuss their merits, but the effect was to antagonize the Tata side even further. Subsequently, the Tatas won both the defamation cases at the Bombay High Court, where I went and argued for them and one of them has been dismissed in the Supreme Court also. The other is pending in the Supreme Court without relief against the Tatas.

Many, many more arguments were raised, as you can imagine, given the interest involved and the importance of the matter. The NCLT heard both sides exhaustively, and then passed a judgement that was 368 pages long. Unsurprisingly, they dismissed the petition filed by Cyrus Mistry's companies in toto. In fact the order was absolutely in favour of Tata Sons.

The key to the NCLT order was that this was in effect a dispute between an employee and an employer, and not between a minority and a majority shareholder. The NCLT came down heavily in favour of corporate democracy – that the will of the majority of shareholders cannot be held to ransom by a minority on such issues which are bona fide business decisions.

On each of the allegations that were raised by Cyrus Mistry, the Court summarily concluded that it found no merit in the claims made. In fact, the Court went one step further and reprimanded him for providing information to the Income Tax Department as being an action contrary to the interest of the company.

According to the NCLT, the most important thing was that the parties that had petitioned the NCLT, being the Shapoorji Pallonji companies, were not impacted as Tata shareholders. Their stake was never sought to be diminished or taken away. No issue of shares was carried out behind their backs. They were not deprived of notices to meetings. No notice to acquire their shares was given to them. Their share values were not driven into the ground. The company was not stripped of assets and sold to turn a quick buck. These are the traditional crimes of oppression and mismanagement, and they never happened. It is not oppression and mismanagement to fire an employee from a position.

Ultimately, this need not have become an issue of pride and could have been settled simply. By pushing the dispute, Cyrus Mistry lowered the price of Tata Sons shares. He controls 18.4 per cent of those shares. The shares controlled by him are worth many billions. The harm he has caused to himself is incalculable. He is the scion of the Shapoorji Pallonji empire, the largest shareholders in Tata Sons. By settling the dispute he would have always been in an advantageous position. Had he played his cards well and with more humility, he would have been the number one man in both the groups of companies.

However, now the matter has travelled to the NCLAT, to be finally decided in appeal. Once more, a valiant effort was made to get an interim stay of the effect of the NCLT's order. But we succeeded in preventing that symbolic victory as well. The final order took over a year after conclusion of arguments in coming.

I can now admit that we were caught in a sticky position. While the NCLT judgement was thumpingly in our favour, it was poorly written and therefore gave us some anxiety at the appellate court. One of the worst positions for a counsel to be in is to be defending a judgement in your favour, but which has weaknesses – the rug might be swept out from under your feet at any time.

The judgement was over-effusive despite being legally sound. It was nothing but poetic and literary licence on the part of the judge, but in the wrong court of appeal, it might appear excessive. That was the only concern we had.

The NCLAT made a lot of comments in court about the language and the form of the NCLT judgement, and it came to within an inch of a possible stay this time. But thankfully the appellate tribunal appreciated that the language did not undermine the legal sense of the judgement and did not stay it. The whole thing was reargued before the appellate court, and was reversed by NCLAT days before this books went to press. More on this at the end of this chapter.

One hopes that the parties can find an end to this issue. But it illuminates one thing for me. One would think perhaps that these fights are very antiseptic and technical, balance sheet–driven affairs. Nothing could be further from the truth. Indian business is still very much centred around family and friends – and when family and friends fight each other, the undercurrents often run much deeper than what is apparently on the table.

Look at our histories. Stories of brothers fighting brothers and friends turning against each other have an ancient Indian heritage, running back to the Pandavas and Kauravas in the Mahabharata, or in Mughal times, the struggle between Aurangzeb and Dara Shukoh for the throne of India. What was true then is true now. Empires are won and lost on pride and personal insult.

PS: As this book was being readied for press, the NCLAT pronounced its judgement (on 18 December 2019). It reversed the order of the NCLT completely, and reinstated Cyrus Mistry to his former position. As the judgement had been pronounced during Supreme Court vacations, at my request, the appellate tribunal suspended the direction to reinstate Mistry as chairman of Tata Sons to allow Tata Sons to approach the Supreme Court in appeal. In the first week of January 2020, despite Mistry's lawyers' vociferous arguments, the Supreme Court gave a full stay on the NCLAT order, observing that they prima facie found the NCLAT judgement highly questionable since it gave the relief of the reinstatement to Mistry which had been expressly given up by him.

7

Aaya Ram Gaya Ram

The Inside Story of Uttarakhand and Karnataka

I have faced all kinds of unusual courtroom scenes in my career, but perhaps nothing so strange as having to argue all night in the Supreme Court. The day will go down in legal history as one of only three times that the highest court in the land opened its doors at night and worked till dawn. In the other two instances, a man was to be hanged in the morning – but both those earlier cases lasted a fraction of the four hours of the night that Karnataka did.

In 2016 and 2018 I was responsible for arguing two major cases which would save Congress state governments in Uttarakhand and Karnataka. It was during the 2018 Karnataka battle that we had the all-night court session. Oddly enough, I had been preparing for those arguments for a very long time.

The topic of my PhD from Trinity College, Cambridge, in 1985, which I did under the guidance of the legendary professor Sir H.W.R. Wade, was emergency powers – the rules under which the normal functioning of a democracy can be suspended. It would have amazed me as a young graduate student to know that one day I would be involved in the rise and fall of multiple governments. That what I was studying would ultimately become the basis for arguments I would make in the future, ones that would end up saving or toppling governments.

Emergency powers have always existed, and do so in most democracies – they are mostly invoked in wartime. The Roman republic, for example, made provisions in its law for a 'dictator', a word which now has only negative connotations but in that era was associated with benevolence. A Roman dictator was a man who was universally respected, a hero, who could be appointed by the Senate to take over decision-making during emergencies such as war or insurrection and to set aberrations right. He would have to surrender his powers after a predetermined period of time, in sixty or ninety days.

Emergency provisions also exist in the United Kingdom and the United States – both Winston Churchill and Abraham Lincoln used them widely in their times. In those countries, the context for the use of these powers is usually wartime.

They exist in our constitutional scheme as well. The President may declare an emergency for the whole of India or any state in wartime. What is unusual is that he may also do so in peacetime if he believes, on the advice of his representative, the Governor of the state, that the normal constitutional order in a particular state has broken down.

When he imposes President's rule, he assumes the power of that state's government for a brief period. In practice, the President is the Central government – he is advised by the prime minister and the Cabinet of ministers and must listen to them. In effect, during President's rule, the Union becomes supreme temporarily. The federal structure, where state governments have their own separate powers, where the Centre cannot intervene, converts into a unitary one overnight.

Naturally, the decision to impose President's rule needs to be properly thought out and it should be taken only rarely. But who is to say that the decision was taken correctly? Whose discretion is final? If the President is satisfied that it is necessary, is that not good enough? Or can a court check whether the decision was correctly taken? In other words, is it open to judicial review, and if so in what circumstances?

Uttarakhand

That was the question before the Uttarakhand High Court, which is housed in a beautiful old building in Nainital. For a few weeks in the spring of 2016, it was one of the most hotly contested battlefields in the country with the cream of the legal fraternity flocking to it.

In 2016 there was a Congress government in place in Uttarakhand, although one with a thin majority, headed by Chief Minister Harish Chandra Rawat. Of seventy-one members of the Legislative Assembly (MLAs), thirty-two belonged to the Congress, twenty-six to the BJP and the rest belonged to other parties.

The budget session for the year started on 9 March, and on the 18th the Appropriation Bill – which is the equivalent of a budget in a state – was taken up for consideration. The bill was passed with a voice vote with the understanding that the majority party had proposed it – and the Speaker noted it as so.

After the bill had been passed, the twenty-six BJP MLAs and nine defector MLAs from the Congress switched allegiances on the bill. These defectors, or rebel MLAs, sought a division of vote, which is a revote by a show of hands. The new BJP side was now apparently in the majority.

The Speaker denied the MLAs a division vote. The Speaker in a legislature has certain rights – he is the one who decides whether a bill has been passed. He is also the correct authority to determine whether a defection has taken place – which entitles him to disqualify defecting MLAs.

The twenty-six BJP MLAs and the nine rebel Congress MLAs went to the Governor's House – Raj Bhavan – on the same day and submitted a signed joint memorandum on the letterhead of the leader of the opposition claiming that the government had been reduced to a minority. They criticized the manner in which the vote on the Appropriation Bill was carried out and pleaded that the Uttarakhand government should be dismissed. In effect they also said that the Appropriation Bill had never been passed.

That night, the thirty-three MLAs left for Delhi in a private plane accompanied by the state and national secretaries of the BJP. The rebel MLAs were then put up at the Leela Hotel in Delhi. The next day, the Speaker wrote to the Governor invoking the anti-defection law (which is in the Tenth Schedule to the Constitution) and asking the rebel MLAs why they should not be disqualified.

On the same day, that is, 19 March, the Governor ordered the Uttarakhand government to seek a vote of confidence on the floor of the legislature, no later than 28 March, which was the next scheduled day for the assembly to convene.

The Governor repeated his direction the next day to the chief minister. The chief minister wrote back saying that the session would be reconvened on 28 March and the vote of confidence would be held then.

Why was there all this back and forth on dates, one might ask. Why did the chief minister not request the Speaker to hold a special session immediately? Also, why was the Governor insistent on it being conducted at the earliest?

The answer lies in the status of the nine rebel MLAs. In short, would their votes count? If their votes counted after they had switched allegiance, were they betraying the voters who had elected them?

In multiparty democracies, citizens tend to vote for the party they prefer, and not so much for the candidate standing. In the late 1960s and early 1970s, a number of governments collapsed because of defections – an MLA who was promised office, or some other lure, would leave his party for another, and as a result the party in power would not have enough seats to continue and the government would fall. One legislator named Gaya Lal changed his party three times in one fortnight, and lent his name permanently to the common phrase about defectors – 'Aaya Ram Gaya Ram'.

To curb this horse-trading, and to disincentivize this obvious corruption in politics, the Constitution was amended in 1985 to include anti-defection provisions, mostly contained in the Tenth Schedule. It essentially said that defections would lead to disqualifications, and the Speaker would be responsible for the decision regarding disqualification.

Parties in the British system and in ours – which is modelled on the Westminster parliamentary system – can direct their members in the house to vote a certain way. This is called a whip. The term historically comes from hunting, and refers to whipping the hounds into a pack, a task which fell to a man called the 'whipper-in'. When a party issues a direction – or a whip – not voting in that way also amounts to defection.

But what about the mind and conscience of the MP/MLA? Suppose my party wants me to vote for something I am against, must I agree? From the perspective of our electoral system, do we vote for parties or persons? Do parties take positions or do persons? Does a legislator lose his freedom of speech and conscience when he takes his position in the house?

The Supreme Court had tested this area of law and had decided in *Kihoto Hollohon*'s case that voting in opposition to the whip should only be called defection where the matters were crucial to the existence of the government or to the electoral programme of the party. Of course, for genuine cases of conscience, the member in question had the right to take prior permission of the party to vote against the direction, and sometimes the party could condone their behaviour.

Returning to our defectors, the proceedings for the disqualification of the nine dissident MLAs were set in motion. Those rebel MLAs approached the Uttarakhand High Court with a writ petition on 25 March, a Friday, seeking postponement of the disqualification proceedings. The Court, however, did not give them the stay they were seeking – the disqualification proceedings were to take place now on the 27th, a Sunday. Having failed before the Court, the government at the Centre now decided to put into play an unusual plan.

A Cabinet meeting was held in New Delhi at 9.30 p.m. on the 26th, crucially scheduled a day before the disqualification hearing already fixed for the 27th, after the result of the Court hearing. A video emerged allegedly dated 26 March, which was apparently doctored. Based on a sting operation, it seemed to show that the chief minister of Uttarakhand was engaging in horse-trading of his own, and trying to buy seats.

These facts – the video, the division vote having been barred by the Speaker and the letter the BJP MLAs and the rebel MLAs had given to the Governor – led the Union Cabinet to conclude that Saturday, 26th night that the constitutional machinery in the state of Uttarakhand had failed.

The Union Cabinet recommended President's rule under Article 356 and the President approved it on Sunday, 27 March. Thereafter, the entire state government was relieved of its powers. In the meantime, the nine rebel MLAs had been disqualified by the Speaker of the Uttarakhand Legislative Assembly. On Monday, 28 March, when the vote of confidence was to take place, there was no legislature in force.

This is where my part in the story truly begins. I appeared for Chief Minister Harish Chandra Rawat in the Uttarakhand High Court, challenging the Central government's invocation of emergency powers under Article 356.

Nainital is one of the more difficult High Courts to get to. One has to fly to Jolly Grant Airport at Dehradun, and from there one can either take a helicopter or go on a very long drive, or do a combination of train and drive. Alternatively, one can take a Delhi–Pantnagar flight, followed by a Pantnagar–Nainital helicopter hop or a Pantnagar–Nainital drive. That road trip takes three hours, and the helicopter hop is only fifteen minutes long. I ended up trying all these combinations at some point or another during this matter.

It became clear that Mr Modi's BJP government sensed an imminent change of government in Uttarakhand and felt that they should have that change at any cost, including by winning over a few more disgruntled MLAs.

Therefore, extraordinarily for a matter at the High Court level, they flew in their then Attorney General Mukul Rohatgi, then Additional Solicitor General Tushar Mehta, Additional Solicitor General Maninder

Singh, counsels like C. Aryama Sundaram, Harish Salve and Nalin Kohli plus a battery of at least five juniors, all defending the same cause.

Of course, since one cannot have a dozen lawyers appear for one party, they were distributed – one appearing for the Centre, one for each rebel MLA, one for the leader of the opposition, etc. – but all essentially arguing the same set of points. All of them were opposing me in a small High Court like Nainital, which was very unusual to say the least – this would have been a star-studded cast for Court 1 of the Supreme Court on a Monday morning. The one good hotel at Nainital was overflowing.

Initially I thought the matter would not go on for long – it would either be decided against us or stayed in the interim, that is, put into a sort of limbo. I expected and packed for one or at most two days. As it turned out, I had underestimated the size of the battle – it went on for almost a dozen days over a month of frequent trips. I was never there for longer than a few days at a time, but it felt like I had been there for ages.

The experience was utterly chaotic but it was also exhilarating and intellectually satisfying. We had a big fight with high stakes on our hands, in an unusual arena.

Thankfully, I also had the support of Devdutt Kamat, a very competent junior counsel, who has recently also been designated a senior.

Cases become interesting when you are sure that whether you lose or win, you are before an absolutely straight and honest bench in which you have faith. I realized very early on that the division bench hearing the matter at the High Court was ramrod straight, which given the stakes, and the legal firepower pointed at it, was critical. The Chief Justice of the Uttarakhand High Court, Justice K.M. Joseph, had a deep interest in the intellectual development of the law. He had even come to the matter having read the main judgements in advance – a rare thing.

I pressed my arguments. First, I went through the facts in great detail, and laid out the events that had occurred between 25 and 27 March 2016, in essence, the span of just one weekend. My narrative showed clearly that the decision to impose President's rule did not come from any of the facts on the ground in Uttarakhand, but was part of a larger pattern of manipulation from the government at the Centre. Something similar had been attempted in Arunachal Pradesh a little earlier. The very basis of the imposition of President's rule, I argued, arose from an ulterior motive.

Second, the decision of the President is fully judicially reviewable. Since the landmark case of S.R. Bommai in 1994, the President needed to have information that would allow him to conclude that the state government could not be carried on in accordance with the Constitution. But did the facts on the ground allow for such a conclusion? What was the basis of his decision?

Both the decisions to hold a vote, and how, and the potential disqualification of the rebel MLAs were the Speaker's decisions to take. The Speaker had already guaranteed a floor test – a vote as to whether the government enjoyed confidence or not. Once the Speaker has put a date for that vote, the regular legislative process is under way.

The only instability was that the rebel MLAs were disqualified before the floor test. That too was a decision in the domain of the Speaker – and the subject of very specific constitutional provisions. In short, while the politics in Uttarakhand appeared shaky, the crisis was being dealt with adequately using the powers vested in the Parliament and with the Speaker. Emergency powers were not needed.

I also stressed that this video – which conveniently

appeared before the Cabinet exactly on the night of 26 March, after the High Court had refused to grant a stay, and shortly before material was to be placed before the President – was obviously doctored and had not been forensically tested.

Often when I am arguing, I turn the perspective around for the Court. Even if, I argued, the Speaker had erred about the division vote on 18 March, could that amount to a trigger for President's rule, particularly when the remedy of a floor test had already been put in motion? Could not the matter have waited ten more days to be determined finally and certainly on the floor of the house and not by Central intervention?

Federalism – the autonomy of state governments, the will of the people to decide in their local and state units how they will be governed – and consequently democracy would be weakened by a decision such as this. I put it that the Governor had acted as a mere postbox instead of applying his mind to the matter before him. How else could a proclamation of President's rule have been made on the flimsy pretext of one mistaken decision?

Third, the Governor had sent eight reports in the preceding week and none of the eight reports of the

Governor had recommended President's rule. He reported all the facts, but not once did he state there was a breakdown of the constitutional machinery. If he had not, what was the motivation for the Cabinet to do so, *apart from bias*?

Mukul Rohatgi, who was leading the arguments for the government, as Attorney General for India, argued two points. One that it was not for the Court to look at the sufficiency, that is, the merits of the material put before the President, but its existence. He argued that usually the Court does not sit in appeal over minutiae of the President's decisions.

He also argued that the power of the Court was confined to examining whether there *was* any basis for the decision and whether it was broadly relevant. If there is no material or it is wholly irrelevant, the Court might interfere, he conceded, but not otherwise.

But if there were at least *some* relevant points, the fact that some other material was irrelevant would not justify the Court invalidating the action under Article 356. The President has to have the freedom to make up his own mind.

The hair's breadth distinction between existence of relevant material and sufficiency of relevant material was the government's defence, and the point in law. It is not for nothing that constitutional law is such a Talmudic exercise.

Rohatgi also argued that if any member of the house had made the demand, the division of votes, that is, a show of hands, would be mandatory. To deny that, in his words, would be 'a murder of democracy'. By failing to pass the Appropriation Bill on the 18th, the government had already fallen – and so President's rule had become necessary.

He also pointed to the fact that one BJP MLA was undergoing disqualification proceedings for an earlier action, but his case was going slowly, whereas those against the rebel MLAs had gone at a blazing pace and had resulted in disqualification in less than ten days. His claim was that the Speaker had not been acting impartially and had rushed the proceedings that had favoured the Congress government.

Finally, Rohatgi dealt with my argument on the reports of the Governor, arguing that it was not necessary for the President to be told that the machinery had broken down – he had to make that determination himself on the basis of the facts before him. Therefore, it didn't matter that the Governor had never made that statement in his reports.

The Court went through the arguments and the documents in exhaustive detail. After many hearing days, Justice Joseph asked some pointed questions in Court, and within a day the Central government knew it was turning against them. Then, and I am sorry to say it of such an eminent set of counsel, the next two days saw a host of delaying tactics, with the Attorney General himself asking time for instructions.

The Chief Justice said he would not adjourn the case, but if the government could revoke the proclamation, the matter could be put to an end – in short, an honourable path was open at that point to the BJP government to not have an order against them. But admission of defeat would have been too embarrassing at the point, and so the dictation of the judgement was completed. It took three days in open court for Chief Justice Joseph to dictate the judgement.

It concluded that President's rule must be tested on the legitimacy of the decision made by the President. The Court held that a 'legitimate inference must be drawn from the material placed before him which is relevant for the purpose'.

The Court also very wisely and courageously stated that the Constitution is essentially a political document and provisions such as Article 356 have the potential to unsettle the entire constitutional scheme. The exercise of those powers needs to be controlled.

Democracy and federalism are essential features of our Constitution. The power given to the President but which is actually in the hands of the Union Cabinet under Article 356 can alter the federal balance, and suspend the choices made by millions of voters.

The power to declare President's rule has the ability 'to emasculate the two basic features of the Constitution and hence it is necessary to scrutinise the material on the basis of which the advice is given and the President forms his satisfaction more closely and circumspectly'.

The Court found that the evidence before the President was irrelevant to the decision he was to take, and none of it could be taken at face value. Further, if it looked like the government was losing support, the only true remedy was the floor test. The only exception to this is if there was a collapse of law and order, and it became impossible to hold a fair floor test.

The Court came down heavily on the government for short-circuiting this process. The Central government had shown bias in favour of its own party and the Court did not hesitate to state as much.

The High Court then made its meaning absolutely clear:

This means that, what was hotly contested before us by the Attorney General on the basis of there being laxity on the part of the Speaker reflecting double standards and also opening the doors to action under Article 356, was without any basis at all. It was a completely non-existent material. There was, in other words, no material. We are, in fact, shocked that the decision taken at the highest level and the matter, which, apparently, influenced the decision, and which engaged the counsel and the Court in this litigation, has been done without due care and without any basis. It was totally without any factual foundation. It was, in fact, a blatant falsehood.

We are of the view that this is a case where all cannons of propriety were thrown to wind and the undue haste made by the Governor in inviting the President to issue the Proclamation under Article 356(1) clearly smacked of mala fides. The Proclamation issued by the President on the basis of the said report of the Governor and in the circumstances so obtaining, therefore, equally suffered from mala fides. A duly constituted Ministry was dismissed on the basis of material which was neither tested nor allowed to be tested and was no more than the ipse dixit of the Governor. The action of the Governor was more objectionable since as a high constitutional functionary, he was expected to conduct himself more fairly, cautiously and circumspectly. Instead, it appears that the Governor was in a hurry to dismiss the Ministry and dissolve the Assembly. The Proclamation having been based on the said report and so-called other information which is not disclosed, was therefore liable to be struck down.

The Court then quashed the proclamation of President's rule, revived the Congress government, and directed that there would be a floor test at the earliest, on 29 April 2016.

The matter went up to the Supreme Court, and the Supreme Court reaffirmed the direction of the High Court. The Centre's legal team managed to delay the matter somewhat, but ultimately the High Court order was upheld by the Apex Court. At that stage, the proclamation was revoked by the Centre.

The Congress government had won a clear majority and continued for the next three years completing its term. It was a matter of great personal satisfaction that I played a role in this. There was, however, one unhappy outcome. When the Chief Justice of Uttarakhand was to be elevated to the Supreme Court, the Central government raised objections and sat on the recommendation, causing considerable delay and adversely affecting his relative seniority at the Court. That was a petty act of revenge, but as befits a great judge, he is now at the Apex Court.

Karnataka

Something very similar happened in Karnataka only a couple of years later. It was May 2018. That day, I happened to be arguing a case in Chandigarh. Even before my matter was taken up, I got a call from Randeep Surjewala, the Congress spokesperson. There was a crisis brewing in Karnataka.

The state elections had just taken place and there was a hung assembly with the BJP getting the most seats (104 out of 224) but not attaining majority. The Congress had taken eighty and the Janata Dal (Secular) had taken thirty-seven, and immediately formed an alliance.

As no one party had a clear majority, the rule was that the single largest 'proven combination' of parties would form the government, and then prove its majority on the floor of the house. Only upon such proven combination failing would the single largest party be invited to form the government.

At eleven that very morning, the BJP MLAs of Karnataka had gone to give their papers to the Governor to form the government despite the fact that a post-election alliance of the Congress and JD(S) was in existence, and had already made their intention clear to him.

The Governor had turned the Congress–JD(S) coalition away and invited the BJP to form the government. The BJP's B.S. Yediyurappa was to be sworn in as chief minister the very next day, that is, on Thursday. The party would then have a full fifteen days before the trust vote, by which time it was expected that they would form the needed numbers through defections or alliances.

As luck would have it, Chandigarh airport was shut for repairs that day. If I took the train, I would have reached Delhi only at night. But then I remembered that there was an airstrip at Pinjore, and asked Randeep to send a jet to pick me up. In the meantime, as I scrambled to get back to Delhi, Devdutt Kamat, who knew this type of case well and had worked with me in Uttarakhand, was, under my telephonic instructions, already drafting our petition to the Supreme Court.

My matter at Chandigarh finished at one o'clock, and I drove straight to Pinjore and reached there around three o'clock. My plane was waiting with the engines on. By the time I landed in Delhi it was already 5 p.m., well after the usual closing time of four for the Supreme Court.

By about 7 p.m., Devdutt Kamat was before the Registrar seeking an urgent listing, which was incredibly unlikely. However good and urgent our case may have been, the Court does not sit at night. It looked like we had missed our chance to be heard before the swearing-in on Thursday morning.

I landed and the Congress party convened an emergency meeting at our power centre. I was already tired after my hectic day. It was hot, the peak of summer. But from wherever they were in the country, the top leaders of the Congress had assembled: P. Chidambaram, Kapil Sibal, Ahmed Patel, Anand Sharma and Randeep Surjewala were ready to strategize in a matter of hours.

183

I remember wondering to myself, why do people think the Congress machinery is slow?

It was decided that Chidambaram and Sibal would take the press conferences, and I would prepare the case with Devdutt. Devdutt and I spoke over the phone as I went home. He had hit a dead end with the Registrar of the Supreme Court. Very understandably, the Registrar was of the view that the matter could wait till morning.

On my advice, Devdutt kept at it heroically, explaining the consequences and the reasons for why the matter must be taken up at night. Finally, the Registrar agreed to take the case to the Chief Justice to ask if he would consider a night hearing in such unusual circumstances.

I take my hat off to Justice Dipak Misra, who could easily have said we should come in the morning – this would have been reasonable. But he began to think seriously about whether our case could be heard immediately and a bench assembled at night.

I had an inkling that it could happen by about 9 p.m., and told Devdutt and all my juniors to stay at the Court. Although there was no confirmation, I decided around 10 p.m. that I should be close to the Supreme Court premises, because there was the sliver of a chance. So at 11 p.m. I put on my court clothes, gathered my band and gown, and headed to the Taj Man Singh for a cup of coffee, and some more waiting.

Somehow, the media had got wind of the developments; they were outside my house waiting for me to leave. It was a surreal moment, to be dressed for court shortly before midnight. At midnight, as I was having my second cup of coffee, I got a call saying the bench would sit after all. Leaving my coffee, I rushed to court.

At 1.45 a.m., as most of India slept, we began this extraordinary hearing. The bench was Justice A.K. Sikri, Justice S.A. Bobde and Justice Ashok Bhushan, a bench of wise and balanced judges. There was a crowd in the Court as large as the ones in the day. The press was there in force as well. I found out later that my wife had been up all night watching the case live on TV. I opened my arguments.

From 1.45 to 4 a.m., roughly for two hours, the bench was largely against me, in an intellectual and legal sense, taking the view that even if I had a case, there were too many technicalities in the way. But I persisted, showing them the case law, as it had developed, and the facts. Always the facts.

The fact was the Congress and JD(S) had gone to the Governor first and submitted their papers on 15

May. The fact was that there was a clear majority of the Congress–JD(S) combination. The fact was that the Governor denied their claim for no valid reason, and kept them pending. The fact was that the next day, on 16 May, the Governor immediately assented to the BJP, even though they had obviously and admittedly fewer seats, and invited them to form the government.

The fact was that the Congress–JD(S) list of names and signatures of the MLAs in support was before the Governor, showing a majority of 116 out of 224 seats, and the Governor still issued a letter to the BJP to form government, even though the BJP claim was made later. The bias was evident from even the narration of facts. Attorney General Venugopal raised a number of technical arguments and went deep into the rulebook, but ultimately the unfairness of the facts would go against him.

I finally turned the bench at four o'clock in the morning. They had physically put the file down and were ready to dismiss the case. Justice Bhushan turned first, when it became clear there was really no other way to read the facts. Justice Sikri turned second. And then they convinced Justice Bobde.

They did not give me everything I had prayed for.

No stay on the swearing-in was forthcoming, but they said three very important things. First, that the outcome of the election and the Governor's decision would be subject to the petition, which meant that there would be no permanence to the swearing-in.

Second, I had insisted that, ultimately in all these questions, we must fall back on the gold standard of the parliamentary floor test. I submitted that the only right thing was that the Court order the floor test the very next day, to prevent horse-trading. If I had asked for any more time, the Court would have doubted the alliance's majority. When we ourselves were willing to have it at that moment, even on a Saturday, they realized that the numbers in favour of the Congress–JD(S) combination were clear.

Rohatgi, appearing for the BJP, kept insisting on the two weeks that the Governor had given the BJP, and then made the fatal mistake of reducing the days they needed from fifteen to ten to seven, each time demonstrating that their side did not have the numbers at hand. It is always likely that where you do not have a majority, and you are claiming it, you intend to buy that majority.

The third thing the Court decided, which was

critical, was to hear the case finally as soon as possible. The judges said the matter would be decided on Friday morning. Very hopefully, I asked them to list it on Thursday morning, and the judges laughed. Justice Bobde, I think, said, 'Dr Singhvi, it is already Thursday morning.' And indeed, it was 5 a.m. when we left the Court.

B.S. Yediyurappa was sworn in at 9 a.m. on Thursday. It was to be a very short tenure. A thing which may have rankled the bench was that Yediyurappa insisted on having the swearing-in on Thursday – somehow thinking that that would make his position permanent. If he had wisely said that he respected the decision of the Court and awaited a final Supreme Court order, it might have helped him. But he tried to pre-empt the Court, which hurt his image.

Even though I got home at dawn bone-tired, I was back in Court three hours later. It happened that one of my first matters was before Justice Sikri and we both looked at each other and had a short laugh. I said, 'Your Lordship must be thinking I am some kind of bad penny, to turn up night and day.'

The Supreme Court finally decided on Friday that the only way to test the majority was a floor test, and a floor test at the earliest. It directed a floor test at 4 p.m. on Saturday, with the swearing-in of each of the large number of newly elected MLAs to start on Saturday morning. To nobody's surprise, the BJP was in a minority, and their government of three days fell.

In 2019 both Uttarakhand and Karnataka became BJP states again, Uttarakhand through clear elections, and Karnataka through yet another saga of defections and floor tests. Later, a similar pattern was seen in Maharashtra with the imposition of President's rule in a hung assembly, and then the rapid stitching together of a majority in very controversial circumstances. The Maharashtra episode took place as this book was being readied for press, but I think it is of sufficient interest to devote a few pages to.

In the Maharashtra Legislative Assembly elections, which were declared in October 2019, once again no single party or pre-poll combination had a clear majority. The BJP had the largest number of seats and were invited to seek support to make up the government. They could not succeed at that. No single party could create a government. President's rule was imposed as no government was forthcoming. Subsequently, a post-poll alliance of the Indian National Congress, the

Shiv Sena and the Nationalist Congress Party (NCP) emerged on 22 November 2019. This alliance worked out an internal arrangement, and was in a clear majority. It approached the Governor, and on the morning of 23 November 2019, Uddhav Thackeray was expected to take his oath as chief minister of Maharashtra. There was no expectation of any foul play.

On the morning of 23 November, India awoke to a strange cognitive dissonance. The newspapers said that Uddhav Thackeray was to take his oath, and yet, on the television, Devendra Fadnavis of the BJP had taken his oath as chief minister. It turned out that at midnight, a BJP-led alliance, bolstered by defectors from the NCP led by Ajit Pawar, had presented their claim to the Governor. The Governor had then sent a recommendation to the President to lift President's rule. In the wee hours of the morning, at five forty-seven, President's rule had been revoked. Subsequently, the Governor had invited a BJP-led alliance to form the government. Devendra Fadnavis took his oath at 8 a.m. The NCP immediately disowned the defectors. There was no believable majority at all.

The Shiv Sena and Congress immediately went to the Supreme Court, notwithstanding that it was a Saturday.

The Supreme Court set up a special bench which sat on Sunday, 24 November, to hear us. Coming straight to the point, the Court asked the Maharashtra government to submit all the documents showing the strength of the alliance, and the documentary basis of the Governor's decision. On Tuesday, 26 November, the Court directed a floor test to be conducted within twenty-four hours. That evening, seeing that the game was up, Devendra Fadnavis and Ajit Pawar resigned.

On 28 November, Uddhav Thackeray took his oath, with a proven majority. The BJP-led government in Maharashtra had lasted three days.

After Maharashtra, I think there are some conclusions I can draw about this set of political adventures. This last and most recent episode shone a light on how this sort of manipulation and gaming of the system casts a doubt on democracy, elected governments and probity in public life.

Personally and professionally, I felt very excited simply because, apart from the intellectual stimulation and job satisfaction that comes from doing great work, I had been the lead counsel on each one of the links in this whole chain of matters, namely, Jharkhand, Goa,

Uttarakhand, Karnataka and Maharashtra. These have all now become precedents for the Court.

The lessons we learnt from Maharashtra are a sort of code for the law on this area. Be you ever so adventurous, so cunning with your political stratagems, the courts will bring you to the direct floor test with the shortest possible time to prove your majority. The only real question is who commands a true majority – what is the will of the people. This period before your majority is tested has become less than forty-eight hours in most cases. The object is to prevent artificial and contrived majorities obtained by unfair means, illegal inducements and coercive pressure. The Court has shown a willingness to sit beyond court hours, through the night, on weekends, even in the predawn, to ensure that democratic governments are preserved. Similarly, the straitjackets of procedure and formality will not be allowed to stand in the way.

The role played by Governors has not escaped the Court's attention. In many of these situations, Governors have acted as yes-men. Governors, however exalted their position under the Constitution, are not beyond judicial scrutiny, and even in the press are subject to public outrage and ridicule. Similarly, it is understood that the

President acting under Article 356 is acting on the aid and advice of the Central government, and, therefore, the courts can test it as they test all government action.

The position of Governor is an interesting one – we have had both political Governors and apolitical Governors in Indian history. When I say apolitical, the term is an arguable one, but I mean renowned academics, globally recognized statesmen and public figures, and domain experts. One would hope that appointing Governors who come from a non-political background would make them less likely to obey a party blindly. But it has not necessarily played out that way. Not every political Governor has acted in his party's interest. It is equally possible for a technocrat or a domain expert to act with servility or bias. Not every apolitical Governor has been truly independent-minded. Needless to say, everything that goes for the Governor goes for the President as well.

If I could go back to my unheated student rooms at Cambridge now, I would be able to tell myself one thing – that the law of judicial review of emergencies would change immeasurably. Article 356 was used about a hundred times between Independence and the year 2000. It was abused a great number of times, including many times, I must concede, by Congress governments.

However, between the year 2000 and the year 2020, we have seen about a dozen uses of the provision – which is due to the fact that the Courts have realized that there must be a decision on the question immediately; otherwise there is no reason to have judicial review. The famous earlier judgements such as *S.R. Bommai* were all ultimately infructuous – they functioned to decide whether President's rule had historically been correctly declared, but many, many years later.

The Courts now are sending the message that they will not only lay down the law, but will try to ensure that nobody gets the benefit of their own wrongdoing. Even between Uttarakhand and Maharashtra, the promptness of judicial correction has increased. So this increasingly telescoping approach is making the invocation and use of these powers rarer and rarer, which is the way it should be, as an emergency power. It is a poor government which makes the exception the rule.

8

The Use and Abuse of Animals

Idgah Slaughterhouse and Jallikattu

You should meet Azlan, my Anatolian shepherd. I think everyone in my family will concede that he is the real head of the family. The export of Anatolian shepherds as a breed, I believe, is banned in Turkey, their place of origin. They really are a national treasure. In the Turkish mountains they say that one dog can guard a herd of a thousand sheep. Azlan came to us from a family in Italy, and he has been the love of my life for the last eleven years – don't tell my wife I said this.

I have always loved animals. I cannot stand to see them mistreated – it hurts me deeply. I also happen to be a Jain. Jains, as you know, abhor violence even to the lowest forms of life, including insects and root vegetables. To us, even a germ, a microscopic life form, is worthy of respect. Animals for us are a very high form of life. As a result, over my career, I have put serious time and effort in protecting animal rights before the Courts.

Animal rights occupy a strange middle ground in our legal system. Many people eat animals. I have no objection to that – dietary habits and choices are a matter of personal freedom. In fact, vegetarians are actually a minority in India – 75 per cent of Indians eat meat occasionally. Of course, compared to countries in western Europe or America, the per capita meat consumption of even an Indian non-vegetarian is relatively small.

The law allows people to kill and eat animals. Animals have also been used since the beginning of history to do labour – humans have domesticated horses, cattle, camels, donkeys, goats, even birds and bees, to do their work. However, we do also have a set of laws including the Prevention of Cruelty to Animals Act, 1960, which makes it punishable by law to cause unnatural pain and suffering to animals.

In effect, however, well-meaning legislations often clash with the realities of commercial interests, embedded traditions and habits and patterns, which are harder to change than legislatures imagine. When people don't want to follow a law, it is very hard for the government to enforce it, and the findings of right and wrong become slightly academic.

Our laws control and regulate even animal slaughter so that it is done as humanely as possible. It is, of course, worth noting that different communities have different traditions of animal slaughter. For example, Jews follow a procedure which ensures that meat is kosher, and Muslims traditionally consume meat which is halal.

The practice of animal slaughter, however, can raise some difficult questions. One of the matters I remember best was the famous Idgah slaughterhouse case – *Maneka Gandhi* v. *Union Territory of Delhi & Ors.*

In the early 1990s the biggest slaughterhouse in Delhi was the Idgah slaughterhouse, located in Sadar Bazaar. The Idgah slaughterhouse had long been an issue of public hygiene and safety. It had been built around the turn of the nineteenth century when the population of Delhi was a fraction of what it was in 1990. Delhi in 1900 was a city of around four lakh people. By 1990, it was a megacity of almost one crore people.

The slaughterhouse, however, had remained much the same. In fact, instead of expanding, its premises had shrunk because of encroachment. Every day, hundreds of thousands of animals were brought to the Idgah slaughterhouse and killed. The area had become densely populated, and the roads to the slaughterhouse were very narrow. Adjacent to the slaughterhouse were three schools, and thousands of children studied there.

Slaughtering is a messy business and if it is to be done in a hygienic manner, it requires a lot of space. The Idgah slaughterhouse, which was overseen by the Municipal Corporation of Delhi, had become horrifically cramped. As a result, the streets outside were filled with animal dung, urine and blood. Visitors to the area were repulsed by what they saw.

The abattoir and street outside was ankle-deep in filth and entrails. Animals were brought in cramped by the truckloads, and meat was carried out in rickshaws, on the backs of workers, uncovered, unpackaged. The meat was not being tested for diseases. Animals were not rested or separated for the slaughter and were screaming with fear. The water supply of the area was contaminated.

But still, this was the centre of the meat trade for the city of Delhi and millions derived their daily food from the meat slaughtered here. Thousands worked at the slaughterhouse, and their families were dependent on their income. There was no other place for the slaughtering of animals in Delhi, and so it continued.

Maneka Gandhi approached the Supreme Court about the matter. The Supreme Court directed the Delhi High Court to hear the matter urgently. The High Court, in the interest of the public, reduced the number of animals being slaughtered daily to 2500 only. The Municipal Corporation of Delhi was also directed to take steps to improve the situation and clean up the slaughterhouse area.

The Buffalo Traders Association and other associations from the meat industry appealed to the Supreme Court, which set up a committee to investigate issues and report back to the Court.

I was a young counsel around that time – I had only recently become a senior advocate. I was briefed by the Akhil Bharat Krishi Go Sewa Sangh, an animal rights organization, and was present before the Delhi High Court in 1995.

The crux of the matter was not really a tidy legal question – one of two conflicting rights – but a messy question of implementation. We all knew that the slaughterhouse was unsanitary and overburdened and could not be permitted to continue in the heart of the city, where it was causing pollution and could potentially result in health issues for huge numbers of people, including first and foremost consumers of the meat slaughtered there.

On the other hand, this was the historical centre of a very large industry, and there was no second location in existence in Delhi. What would happen to thousands of unemployed workers if the slaughterhouse was shut down?

What followed was a crusade to shift the slaughtering to a more suitable place and create a new, modern slaughterhouse along scientific lines. But this would entail public expense. One of the major fighters in the crusade was lower court law officer C.K. Chaturvedi, who took it on himself to combat the vested interests who were opposed to any change.

One thing I think I can say quite clearly. If this issue had arisen in the present day, in 2019, it would have been given a very ugly communal colour, and the politicians we have now would have exacerbated and escalated the issue. The majority of the employees and the immediate stakeholders were Muslim, and many of those protesting the situation were Hindu. The communal issue existed in the 1990s but in a much more muted way. It is sad that a municipal cleanliness issue, a cruelty issue, would almost certainly today be mischaracterized and conflated into a religious issue. This is a sad comment on recent developments in our republic.

My instructions were coming to me from a number of organizations that were religious in nature. There was my main party, the Akhil Bharat Krishi Go Sewa Sangh. Apart from my immediate clients, there were a number of Jain organizations that thought I had taken up the matter because I was a Jain. All of them pressed me to seek an absolute ban on the slaughter of animals in Delhi. With all of them, I was resolute and clear.

It was not for anyone to instruct citizens as to whether they should be vegetarian or not. The object, I reasoned with them, was to ensure that the slaughter being conducted was carried out in the most environmentally sound, cruelty-free and hygienic manner possible. I think perhaps the parties I was appearing for were taken aback, as they thought that being a Jain, I would take a strident position. But as a counsel one must be reasonable and must respect the Constitution and law – we have a duty to be fair.

That was the middle path we pursued and it stood us in good stead. It was also why the issue did not acquire an unnecessary communal colour. The committee was split almost exactly down the middle, with half wanting to keep the number of animals slaughtered to the number mandated by the Supreme Court and the other half wanting to increase it.

My clients thought the reduction was necessary, and that in the long run the slaughterhouse would have to be shifted. The meat traders' association wanted to increase the number of animals slaughtered from 2500 to at least 7500, which they argued was still lower than the original.

The Buffalo Traders Association and meat lobby raised the following arguments:

(1) They argued that the Idgah slaughterhouse could actually take an increased capacity. They showed a basis for saying that 5000 sheep or goats a day and an additional 2500 buffaloes, or 6000 sheep or goats and 1500 buffaloes could be slaughtered hygienically.

(2) The abattoir actually generated a great deal of foreign exchange earning because the meat that was slaughtered there was exported as well.

(3) Since the schools had come much later, they should be shifted and not the abattoir.

(4) Traders have a fundamental right to carry on their trade, and animal slaughter is permissible in law.

(5) If the municipality was not going to permit slaughtering at the slaughterhouse, then private slaughterhouses must be permitted.

Thankfully, the NGOs that had been working with me had studied the process of transporting and slaughtering animals thoroughly, and they briefed me on the facts. That research was useful because I could present facts and figures that the Court could not overlook. The arguments I took up were the following:

(1) While the Municipal Corporation of Delhi had in the meantime spent a lot of money to try to improve the Idgah slaughterhouse, there was a limit to the improvement because there was simply not enough space, and it was located in the heart of the densest part of the city.

(2) The space at the Idgah slaughterhouse was in fact insufficient even for 2500 animals.

(3) The traffic in the area was unimaginable and the slaughterhouse would need about 862 trucks to transport 2500 animals.

(4) More than 8000 boys and girls were studying in the schools surrounding the slaughterhouse, and have to make their passage through that area daily.

(5) Both ante-mortem and post-mortem examinations should be conducted on the animals to make sure they are not diseased. Those diseases can be transmitted to the consumers of the meat as well. These examinations would only be possible when the numbers were restricted – and if numbers were increased in the circumstances as they were, those examinations would simply not be conducted.

(6) Animals are brought from far to Delhi to be slaughtered. They come from Rajasthan, Uttar Pradesh, Madhya Pradesh, Haryana and Gujarat. The travel is stressful on the animals and they ought to be transported in a cruelty-free manner. The stress lowered the quality of the meat as well.

(7) I stressed the importance of lairage, which is internationally understood to be necessary. Lairage is the resting of animals prior to slaughter, keeping them calm and relaxed, and separating them from the animals being slaughtered, which causes them fear. The animals needed to be rested for at least twenty-four hours and there was just no space for that.

(8) The air and water pollution caused by the slaughterhouse needed to be taken into account. Samples showed that the water in the area was exceedingly polluted. In fact,

the Pollution Control Board had already issued warnings to the slaughterhouse to start effluent treatment or shut down.

(9) Illegal slaughtering by private parties has been going on for a while, at places other than the abattoir, and in vast quantities, because the Idgah slaughterhouse was under so much pressure. This had to be checked.

(10) There was simply no way to let the Idgah slaughterhouse continue – the pollution and the surroundings were more than sufficient to mandate its closure. The fact was simply that it was a facility created when Delhi had a population of four or five lakh, not ninety-two lakh.

To my mind, as necessary as a slaughterhouse was, it needed to be located on the edge of the city, in a zone with very little population density, and not in the heart of it. These are historical remnants – when the slaughterhouse was built, it was not a problem, but the city was very different then.

To take another example, Kanpur is known for its leather industry, which is very polluting. The industry started and the city grew around it. But such a noxious industry cannot be run in the heart of the city today.

The Court agreed with us completely. It held that

the government should set up a large, modern facility at the earliest and that the Idgah slaughterhouse should be closed by the end of 1995. The government was also directed to ensure that those made redundant would be rehabilitated and given employment elsewhere.

The authorities, however, dragged their feet a long time. The shifting was prolonged and extended, and vested interests delayed it as much as possible. The Municipal Corporation of Delhi was a divided house. Some were in favour of the shift being carried out at the earliest, and some were clearly influenced by the vested interests. As a result, it went much slower than it should have.

The Supreme Court restricted the slaughter to 2000 goats or sheep a day and extended the period of the Idgah slaughterhouse's functioning to the end of June 1997. Then it was extended again and again because the new facilities had yet to be built

It was only in 2009 that the Idgah slaughterhouse was finally shut down, since replaced by a much improved slaughterhouse in Ghazipur. The neighbourhood has improved greatly for it. In a society where many people eat meat, there must be slaughter. But as a society we can hope that slaughter is done as humanely as possible.

An update to that episode is the question of battery farming chickens, which is pending before the Supreme Court right now. I am appearing for animal rights groups seeking to have the practice of raising chickens in these inhuman conditions deemed cruel and illegal. Of course, we are opposed by very powerful commercial interests, and will have to fight hard. But anyone who has seen how chickens are raised right now will know that there must be a more humane way of treating them.

~

Twenty years later, and at the other corner of the country, we came across yet another fascinating case where the rights of animals were tested. In Tamil Nadu, there exists a traditional form of entertainment called Jallikattu, which has a strong folk following. Jallikattu has ancient origins and is almost a kind of bullfighting, except that it is not intended to be lethal to the bull. It occurred at the end of the harvest season, in January and February, alongside the temple festivals.

The word itself comes from 'calli', meaning coins, and 'kattu' meaning package. Historically, a package of coins would be tied to the horns of a fearsome bull, and it would be considered an act of courage to pluck it from its horns. Over time, that evolved into a set of sports which include corralling an enraged bull, racing it, trying to control it, etc.

The problem with Jallikattu, which may otherwise sound innocent, is that in practice it can be very cruel. Bulls are herbivores who graze and stay in herds. They exhibit stress and anxiety when separated from the herd or are put into strange environments. Where they see a perceived threat, they respond with a 'fight or flight' reaction, which is exploited by these sports.

In Jallikattu, the bulls are corralled into cramped wooden enclosures and then forced into a crowd of strange people and noises. In order to force them to charge, they are poked and prodded with knives and sticks, their tails are twisted and bitten, irritants are rubbed into their eyes, and they are yanked by nose ropes.

They are frequently starved of food and water, but shortly before the event, they are forced to drink liquor. Then once they charge, they are lassoed by teams of men and dragged by their nostrils to a tree. In the course of this practice, the bulls frequently break loose, run into roads and wells, break their legs and, of course, can cause immense injuries to humans, sometimes ending in their deaths.

Bulls are not designed to run for more than the shortest of distances. Their hooves cannot take the weight of such a heavy body landing on two legs – unlike, say, a horse. Therefore, a bull has to literally be whipped into racing.

The matter came to the Supreme Court on a couple of very interesting points. Tamil Nadu had enacted a law called the Tamil Nadu Regulation of Jallikattu Act, 2009, which permitted the sport while regulating it nominally. In the meantime, there had been a notification put out by the Ministry of Environment and Forest banning the use of animals including bulls for such performances. However, it had exempted Jallikattu from the ban seeing as it had cultural value.

The Animal Welfare Board of India (AWBI) was created to enforce the Prevention of Cruelty to Animals Act. The AWBI and People for the Ethical Treatment of Animals (PETA) challenged the Tamil Nadu Regulation of Jallikattu Act before the Madurai bench of the Madras High Court. From the other side, a petition before the Bombay High Court challenged the ban on bull racing. These cases were all writ petitions, where the government was the respondent, asked to justify the positions it had taken. Both of these together came up to the Supreme Court under the title *Animal Welfare Board of India* v. *A. Nagaraja*.

The AWBI argued that Jallikattu was a cruel practice and had to be struck down under the Prevention of Cruelty to Animals Act. Now there is a question here of real interest – if there is already a law permitting the practice and regulating it, such as the Tamil Nadu Regulation of Jallikattu Act, which law will win out?

Under our federal system, both the legislature at the Centre, that is, Parliament, and the legislature at the state level can pass laws. Our Constitution has set out three lists that determine which subjects they are permitted to pass laws about. There are some things which only the Centre can pass laws about, such as foreign policy. These are contained in List I. There are similarly some things which only states can pass laws about, such as policing, and these are contained in List II. In these fields, the state legislature is supreme. There is a third category – List III, the Concurrent List – containing subjects on which both the Centre and the state can pass laws. Of course, if there is any conflict, the Central act prevails.

In principle, whenever a state law conflicts with a Central law, we have to see whether they can be read together so as to assist each other. Lawyers use the dainty term 'harmonious interpretation' for such an exercise. Therefore, if Jallikattu could be done cruelly or not cruelly, meaning that if the Tamil Nadu act made such cruelty illegal, then the Prevention of Cruelty to Animals Act and the Tamil Nadu act could be read together harmoniously.

The Supreme Court ended up holding that in permitting Jallikattu, the Tamil Nadu act necessarily came in conflict with the Prevention of Cruelty to Animals Act. There was no way, the Court held, that Jallikattu could be carried out without cruelty, and therefore without violating the Prevention of Cruelty to Animals Act.

Since an act enacted by a state had come into conflict with a Central act, it was deemed to be bad in law – this concept is called 'repugnancy'. Where both the state and the Centre can make a law on a subject, that is, in the Concurrent List, and there is a disagreement or repugnancy between a state act and a Central act, the Central act will always win out.

As a result, the Tamil Nadu Regulation of Jallikattu

Act was held to be void, the practice of Jallikattu was found to be illegal and punishable under the Prevention of Cruelty to Animals Act, and a very strong precedent for animal rights was laid down.

It is never quite so simple.

The people of Tamil Nadu and Kerala, and the Tamil Nadu government itself, reacted strongly to the judgement. There was tremendous anger from people to whom the tradition was important. A review petition was filed and put up before the Supreme Court. I appeared for the AWBI and other parties.

The state of Tamil Nadu was in a position where it was trying both to defend the practice of Jallikattu and the law it had passed. Shekhar Naphade, senior advocate, appearing for the state, tried to argue a very creative, if desperate, line – that there was no repugnancy at all.

The earlier judgement had found that the power to enact the legislations for both the Centre and the state flowed from Entry 17 in the Concurrent List, being 'Prevention of cruelty to animals'. Therefore, when the Tamil Nadu act was in conflict with the Centre's act, the Central act had to take precedence.

Naphade tried to persuade the Court that the Tamil Nadu act was actually passed in exercise of powers which came from the State List, where there could be no interference from the Centre.

Naphade tried to argue that the relevant powers came from Entries 14 and 15 of the State List which were 'Agriculture, including agricultural education and research, protection against pests and prevention of plant diseases' and 'Preservation, protection and improvement of stock and prevention of animal diseases; veterinary training and practice'. Since there are agricultural roots to the practice, the state was trying to turn the entire matter into a question of agriculture and animal husbandry. This would have kept the matter within the state's jurisdiction.

I argued against this reading, pointing to the very wording of the Tamil Nadu act, which was aimed at controlling Jallikattu and checking excessive cruelty in the practice. Therefore, the matter was most directly connected to the issue of 'prevention of cruelty to animals'.

The Court agreed with me and held that there was really no way to drag the Tamil Nadu act so far from its normal and sensible meaning as to fall under agriculture and preservation of stock.

Legal creativity usually comes from being stuck

in a hard place and Naphade tried to advance yet another intriguing argument. He tried to bring the practice of Jallikattu within the realm of the practice of religion. We have earlier in this book gone over some of the arguments concerning the practise of religion in connection with topics like santhara and temple entry at Sabarimala.

Naphade's argument was that Jallikattu was an essential religious practice, and thus the law could not legitimately restrict it. While this was creative, it was an argument doomed to fail because none of the requirements for it, laid down over more than half a century ago, were met. The practice had no connection with any religion or sect, there was no basis in scripture or a distinct set of believers. The argument was only that the tradition was old, and the harvest festival is one deemed to have roots in religion. The Court brushed aside this argument as well.

The Court went on to agree with its earlier view, and we succeeded again. Much to the disappointment of the state and the proponents of Jallikattu, the bench of Justice Dipak Misra and Justice U.U. Lalit was clear that custom was no reason to justify cruelty, particularly where the law to deal with cruelty is so clear. To pass a judgement in the face of so much media attention, which would almost certainly anger the majority of the people in a part of the country, is an act of courage as well – and at the end of the day, animals cast no votes.

The people of Tamil Nadu, however, erupted in protest. The Supreme Court may have spoken finally, but the decision of the Court was unacceptable to the people.

Unfortunately, thereafter, because of the immense pressure on the government in Tamil Nadu, bulls were removed from the list of animals against whom cruelty is banned through the Prevention of Cruelty to Animals Act by a state amendment. This allowed Tamil Nadu to bypass the Supreme Court judgement. The Centre also assented to the amendment. I was personally pained by the thought of those bulls being deliberately put through so much cruelty, even after we had succeeded in law.

This may strike you as unfair, and you would be right. If a law is enacted to circumvent a decision of the Court, how can it possibly be a good law? The amendment was clearly passed to nullify the judgement of the Supreme Court, and as such was open to challenge.

But there are such things as political realities, and

after the immense protests in favour of Jallikattu in 2017, no political party could be heard to speak out against Jallikattu. The statute was challenged of course, by the AWBI, and I was prepared to appear for them. But I was begged not to by the Congress party in Kerala. They pointed to the vast and widespread support for the practice and beseeched me not to appear.

I refused for a long time but gave in ultimately, in the interests of avoiding controversies and political backlash. I gave up the brief, thinking it would be better not to appear than to appear half-heartedly and having to watch my words. There are many competent counsels who could press the issue. I must say though that this was one of the few occasions on which I have regretted my political limitations.

As a result of the immense backlash and the amendment to the Prevention of Cruelty to Animals Act, Jallikattu continues unabated. I can only hope that there are improvements to the condition of the bulls, and some of the abuses that were happening are being controlled. I believe that the practice as it stands is essentially a cruel one – you cannot do it without cruelty. There is really no way to regulate it at the micro level; either it can be banned or not banned. There was a very strong decision taken by the judiciary, and the executive turned its back on those principles. As I said, animals cast no votes.

Sometimes when one looks at cases like Sabarimala and Jallikattu, what one sees quite clearly are limits to the domain of the law. For someone who has spent a lifetime studying and practising the law, the realization is a heavy one. Who is right? The law passed validly and adjudicated fully? Or the people from whose will the law emanates in the first place?

Conclusion

What you have read is a thin slice of the life of a busy counsel, some of the cases I thought would interest you. This list is very small and selective, and many, many interesting cases have been left out for constraints of space. A small attempt has been made to diversify the nature of the topics. Some of the questions discussed are those which have affected you even if you didn't know it, and some were stories you would have seen in the newspaper and you might have wondered how such a thing came to be. You have now had a ringside seat to a few rounds. You have seen how much of our nation's life runs through the courts, how the Supreme Court's decisions affect so many people's lives.

We are still very much a young democracy, where

the big questions are still in flux. How much will the government interfere in a person's private life? What makes a person a citizen? These questions are still being decided, and the lines are still being freshly laid down.

For a country which is so dependent on its courts, it pains me to say that our court system is not in good health. We have very few judges for very many litigants, and our judges are overburdened. The infrastructure of our trial courts is inadequate, and the quality of trial judges is generally poor. This results in a shameful amount of pendency, and overflowing dockets.

The average High Court judge is looking at a list of more than fifty matters a day – and it requires a superhuman effort for a judge to keep track of so many hundreds of matters a week, to remember the facts, to hear arguments and ultimately to write a well-thought-out, reasoned order which balances the rights and does justice. What happens to the matters which are not heard that day? An adjournment is given for the matter to be heard on some future date.

Adjournments in our system can be crucial, so crucial as to make or destroy cases. Where one party needs urgent relief because their interest is in danger, for example, where a forest is being cut down, the clock is running against that party. When a court says that it will not hear the matter for the next three weeks, there is always the potential for the forest to be absolutely destroyed before the court even adjudicates the question.

Where the clock is ticking against a party, the Court should be conscious and alert to the fact that those questions must absolutely be decided immediately, or some kind of interim protection must be given. Increasingly, there is a tendency to decide hard questions by adjourning them. Once the forest has been cut, no order will bring it back. This is the creation of a fait accompli, and both private and government parties use this tactic ruthlessly.

What disturbs me particularly is how ad hoc procedure has replaced so much of what is laid down in law. The dependence on PILs for the adjudication of large public questions has robbed the Court of the guidance that is offered by procedure. This kind of rule-following is the time-tested wisdom of the law. It is in the certainty of knowing what will or will not happen that the stability of our legal system depends. This is how the historical system of precedent has evolved, and when we call these things 'mere procedure' and put them aside, we risk doing harm to the law.

The Court itself has expanded its powers to include consultative roles, to directing and supervising processes which have been challenged. For example, where the National Register of Citizens (NRC) process in Assam was challenged, the Supreme Court interfered to the extent of acting as the authority itself, laying down procedure. In doing so, it stepped into the realm of the executive. Now the problem becomes, when you want to challenge the process which has been laid down, who will you go to? The Court will be put in the position of deciding whether its own actions were right.

If you recall, we discussed the separation of powers earlier in the book, and how important it is for the judiciary to keep the executive in check and ensure the validity of the laws the legislature passes. The executive has a hand in the appointment of judges, if only (in principle) to an advisory extent. Although it has never been fully necessitated, the legislature can impeach and remove a judge. So far, on the few occasions that impeachment proceedings were started, the judge himself resigned.

Conclusion

The Supreme Court in the past few years, in matters where there are great stakes involved, has shown a reluctance to act against the government. There has always been in courts a tendency to give the government a very long leash, but when it truly matters, the Supreme Court has stepped in to check the government. Across a wide panoply of cases, that is not the case today. Even where it appears that the government has erred, the Court has shown a pattern of deferring, adjourning and otherwise leaving the issue aside until it has lost the importance it had. My fear is that the judiciary has lost some of its independence and the fearlessness that it needs to check the executive and the legislature.

Still there are many parts to a functioning democracy, and issues do not stop with the action of the government or with the judgement of the Court. A free and fearless press, and an active, interested citizenry, with an enquiring mind, are as important to a republic. Ultimately, the duty to scrutinize and uphold the functioning of a democracy rests with the source of its legitimacy and power, which is, you, the people.

THE APP
FOR INDIAN
READERS

Fresh, original books tailored for mobile and for India. Starting at ₹10.

juggernaut.in

1

CRAFTED FOR MOBILE READING

Thought you would never read a book on mobile? Let us prove you wrong.

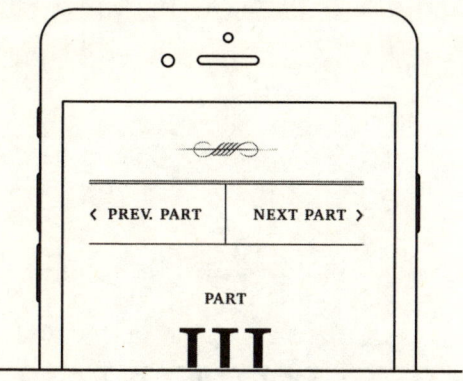

Beautiful Typography

The quality of print transferred
to your mobile. Forget ugly PDFs.

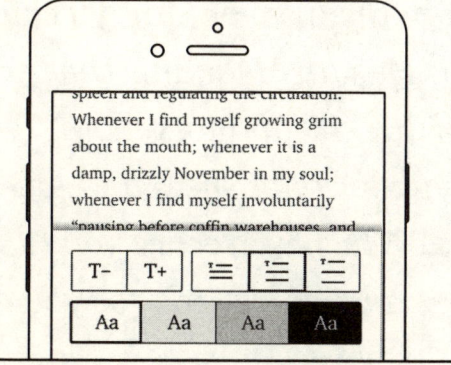

Customizable Reading

Read in the font size, spacing
and background of your liking.

AN EXTENSIVE LIBRARY

Including fresh, new, original Juggernaut books from the likes of Sunny Leone, Praveen Swami, Husain Haqqani, Umera Ahmed, Rujuta Diwekar and lots more. Plus, books from partner publishers and loads of free classics. Whichever genre you like, there's a book waiting for you.

DON'T JUST READ; INTERACT

We're changing the reading experience from passive to active.

Ask authors questions

Get all your answers from the horse's mouth.
Juggernaut authors actually reply to every
question they can.

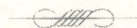

Rate and review

Let everyone know of your favourite reads or
critique the finer points of a book – you will be
heard in a community of like-minded readers.

Gift books to friends

For a book-lover, there's no nicer gift than
a book personally picked. You can even
do it anonymously if you like.

Enjoy new book formats

Discover serials released in parts over
time, picture books including comics,
and story-bundles at discounted rates.
And coming soon, audiobooks.

4

LOWEST PRICES & ONE-TAP BUYING

Books start at ₹10 with regular discounts and free previews.

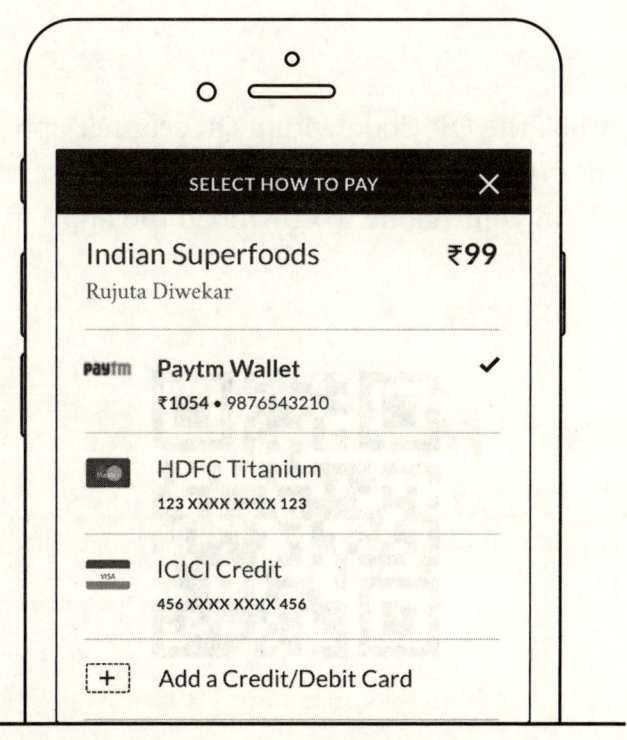

Paytm Wallet, Cards &
Apple Payments

On Android, just add a Paytm Wallet once and buy any book with one tap. On iOS, pay with one tap with your iTunes-linked debit/credit card.

Click the QR Code with a QR scanner app
or type the link into the Internet browser
on your phone to download the app.

For our complete catalogue, visit www.juggernaut.in
To submit your book, send a synopsis and two
sample chapters to books@juggernaut.in
For all other queries, write to contact@juggernaut.in